FEEL HAPPY NOW

FEEL HAPPY NOW

SMALL CHANGES THAT MAKE A HUGE DIFFERENCE

MICHAEL NEILL

HAY HOUSE

Australia • Canada • Hong Kong • India
South Africa • United Kingdom • United States

First published and distributed in the United Kingdom by:
Hay House UK Ltd, 292B Kensal Rd, London W10 5BE. Tel.: (44) 20 8962 1230;
Fax: (44) 20 8962 1239. www.hayhouse.co.uk

Published and distributed in the United States of America by:
Hay House, Inc., PO Box 5100, Carlsbad, CA 92018-5100. Tel.: (1) 760 431 7695
or (800) 654 5126; Fax: (1) 760 431 6948 or (800) 650 5115.
www.hayhouse.com

Published and distributed in Australia by:
Hay House Australia Ltd, 18/36 Ralph St, Alexandria NSW 2015. Tel.: (61) 2 9669
4299; Fax: (61) 2 9669 4144. www.hayhouse.com.au

Published and distributed in the Republic of South Africa by:
Hay House SA (Pty), Ltd, PO Box 990, Witkoppen 2068. Tel./Fax: (27) 11 467
8904. www.hayhouse.co.za

Published and distributed in India by:
Hay House Publishers India, Muskaan Complex, Plot No.3, B-2, Vasant Kunj,
New Delhi – 110 070. Tel.: (91) 11 4176 1620; Fax: (91) 11 4176 1630.
www.hayhouse.co.in

Distributed in Canada by:
Raincoast, 9050 Shaughnessy St, Vancouver, BC V6P 6E5. Tel.: (1) 604 323 7100;
Fax: (1) 604 323 2600

To Mom and Dad and Charlie and Dale
for believing in me when nobody else would
and
to Michael, aged 13 to 20

'This is the true joy in life – the being used for a purpose recognized by yourself as a mighty one; the being thoroughly worn out before you are thrown on the scrap heap; the being a force of Nature instead of a feverish selfish little clod of ailments and grievances complaining that the world will not devote itself to making you happy.'

George Bernard Shaw

CONTENTS

FOREWORD

We are all familiar with the phenomenon of the formidable chore. It may be a closet that needs cleaning or a garage that needs emptying out. We resist the chore like crazy, building up a mountain of reasons why now is not the time and our lives are too full or too busy to take on even one more task.

Then one day, in one moment, we feel differently – and within five minutes the whole job is done. It's not just about how much sugar is flowing through our muscles at any given time that determines our level of activity and interactivity with life. Our consciousness has a power and a rhythm of its own.

The human mind can power the body through a chore (like cleaning closets) when it's in the right mood. And while no one would say that cleaning out a closet is a purely psychological act, the biggest hurdle to getting things done is not in our bodies but in our psyche. It is with the mind that we turn on or off the flow of energy in the body. Yet somehow in our culture today, drugging the brain to alter its chemistry has become unrealistically overemphasised in terms of the role it plays in controlling our moods.

My background, education and work is as a research scientist. While for the past 20 years I have been working on an AIDS drug which is leading to an effective vaccine for the HIV virus, I was originally trained in a neuropharmacology laboratory. We pioneered the development of specific receptor active drugs which increased serotonin and went on to become a new class of highly touted anti-depressants. I was there to watch rapid progress in neuroscience lead to the de-stigmatisation of mental illness, a good thing by any stretch of the imagination.

Yet believe it or not, the popular idea of a 'chemical imbalance' has not been rigorously proven scientifically! Yes, blaming depression on a shortage of serotonin makes a lovely sound-bite for television commercials and pharmaceutical brochures, but the conclusive evidence that anti-depressants work through this mechanism is not actually there. True, important drugs which reverse clinical depression do block the uptake of serotonin into rat brain nerve endings in test tubes. But, to cite but one fly in the ointment, this uptake inhibition happens immediately, while the depression itself doesn't lift for three weeks.

I suspect, based on recent data implicating lipid metabolism in so-called 'bipolar disorder' (a moving target diagnosis which has been changed three times in my professional lifetime), that at its root mental illness is about the rhythm of energy flow throughout the entire body, not in a 'cosmic', mysterious sense, but the amount of actual energy available for our brains and bodies to use.

The idea that you can magically fix a chemical imbalance in the brain with drugs also remains scientifically unproven and the gross over-prescribing of psychoactive drugs is potentially dangerous. As the data has shown, a small percentage of both young people and adults have had severe violent responses towards themselves and others in response to the proliferation of this kind of medication as a 'cure-all' for life's most fundamental problems.

Taking drugs has replaced working on yourself and your life – and now that anti-anxiety and anti-depressant medications can be prescribed by any kind of physician, the lack of counselling and sensitivity to the power of consciousness as a healing force has become endemic.

In sharp contrast to this approach, Michael Neill steps forward in this book as a powerful spokesman for the wonderful world of the mind. He offers clear, practical ways to manage your moods effectively without drugs. These techniques go beyond the traditional offerings of psychotherapy or even cognitive-behavioural therapy and get into the heart of what's possible. There is no mind–body split. There is always something you can do to make things better.

This book also offers a 'happy' alternative to the victim mentality of conventional medical treatment. Through stories of his own battles with depression and the work he has done with clients over the past 16 years, Michael paints a vivid picture of how much of what we feel is actually under our own direct control.

His experience in the realms of thought management through the application of neuro-linguistic programming (NLP) and other cognitive and somatic disciplines is extensive, yet his explanations of how to use these tools to manage your moods quickly and easily are a joy to read and practise. Simply put, we can all learn to make ourselves happy, and this book will show you exactly how to do it.

One caveat:
Clinical depression is a very serious and potentially fatal disease. Neither Michael nor I would argue that you can just will violent or suicidal tendencies away. Anti-depressants can be helpful, even though we don't really know how they work yet. It has been proven that they are most effective when given with therapeutic counselling.

While the techniques in this book are potentially useful even in clinical situations, they will work best in conjunction with a holistic and inclusive approach. Our brains run on sugar (glucose) in a narrow zone of regulation. Therefore the amount of sugar we eat has a profound effect on our moods. At the end of the day, getting to know yourself and how your moods are impacted by the foods you eat and the amount of sleep and exercise you get will form an important part of your personal programme for happiness.

Perhaps I can sum it up best by sharing the story of a young friend of mine whose mother suffered from a diagnosis of bipolar disorder throughout her life. His whole life has been affected by this diagnosis and the widespread belief that he is 'doomed' to inherit unhappiness through his genetic make-up. In fact, there is no clear scientific evidence proving that either depression or anxiety is a genetically transmitted disease.

Yes, stress, anxiety and depression (and for that matter, life itself!) can be extremely difficult to deal with – but the real burden is believing there's nothing you can do about it.

Let's face it – all of us are moody. We may hide our moods in the dark closets of our minds, forcing ourselves to go to work each morning at jobs we don't enjoy and to smile at our colleagues who we don't really know (and who don't really know us). We may even resist the 'chore' of cleaning up our thinking and cleaning up our lives.

And this ultimately leads us to the promise of this practical and important book: when we learn to manage our thoughts and bring love to the front of our mind, that love can override and even transform the 'brain chemistry' which fuels our bodies, our actions and our lives.

Our culture has swung so far to the 'pill for every ill' extreme that I think it is very important for everyone to be exposed to the unique and fresh perspective you are about to discover. Regardless of any academic debate it may cause, I'm going to recommend this book to my young friend. It is clear to me that what Michael Neill has to say works. Read this book, and feel happy!

Candace Pert PhD
Author of *Everything You Need to Know to Feel Good*
www.candacepert.com

Preface

MY STORY

A very learned philosopher dreamed that God appeared to him and offered him the choice between complete knowledge and complete happiness. Being a learned man, he chose complete knowledge. When asked to review what he had learned, he said he realized one thing: he had made the wrong choice.

From the age of 13 until I was around 20, I alternated between depression and mania, barely able to get out of bed on some days and barely able to get back into it on others. My attempts to self-medicate with alcohol, tobacco and other less legal substances never seemed to work for more than a few hours, and as the various cocktails I mixed up inside my body got more elaborate, the feelings (and my ability to deal with them) got worse.

One particularly bad night, while studying at university, I remember collapsing into fits of uncontrollable sobbing in my dorm room. While this was not as unusual an occurrence as I would have liked, this time it was considerably worse, and when the sobbing hadn't stopped by 1 a.m., I recognized that I needed help. I managed to drag myself down to the infirmary, push the 'night call' button and collapse in a heap by the door.

After what seemed like hours but was probably only a few minutes, a night nurse came to the door. She took one look at me and, no doubt ignoring years of nursing training and university protocol, cradled me in her arms and began reciting the Lord's Prayer.

She kept encouraging me to join in, and as I didn't have the energy to explain that I only knew the words because I'd recently played Peter in a deaf-theatre production of *Jesus Christ, Superstar*, I joined in for all I was worth, choking out each line between huge rolling waves of sobbing.

After a few minutes of rocking and praying, the sobbing subsided and I began to feel a sense of peace. Perhaps if I'd been a bit riper for conversion I might have chalked it up to the power of God and converted to Christianity on the spot, but I was still very green in the ways of religion and instead marvelled at this woman's ability to 'love me' back to some modicum of sanity.

She then took me to a doctor's office to wait, assuring me that the doctor would help make me better. The doctor, a fine southern gentleman in his early fifties with thick grey hair and a charming smile, asked me a few questions.

'How long has this been going on?'

'Since I was 13.' I paused, then added encouragingly, 'But only daily for the past month.'

He didn't seem unduly encouraged.

'Come with me.'

He led me down a long hallway, up a short flight of stairs and back down the same hallway on the second floor. It was late and we were seemingly the only ones in the hospital. Opening a door with a set of keys he carried around his neck, the doctor led me into a pristine hospital room and encouraged me to lie down on the bed and rest. Exhausted as

I was from hours of sobbing, that was a very enticing prospect.

'I'll go get something to help you sleep and make you feel better,' he said. 'We'll admit you in the morning.'

When the door shut behind him, I had a moment of incredible clarity – I was at a turning point and my life was about to change forever. In a way, the choice I had to make was simple. If I stayed, I could just hand my brain over to the doctors and let them try to sort it out for me; if I left, I was going to have to find a way of dealing with the feelings that had overcome me like waves for many years.

I opened the door to the hallway, but my nurse friend was now sitting at a desk at the end of the hall. She didn't see me and I didn't have the heart to tell her I was running away. I stepped back into the room and walked over to the window. While the room was on the second floor, the window opened out onto a sort of portico, a mini-rooftop over the mock-Roman colonnades that were all the rage in institutes of higher learning at the time. Gingerly, I opened the window, stepped out onto the roof and jumped the 10 feet or so down to freedom.

While that incident was not the end of my battle with depression, anxiety and stress, it was the beginning of my search for solutions – solutions which can be used by almost anyone to make an immediate difference to your moods, your outlook and your life. I have refined these solutions with my students and clients over the past 16 years and tested each one of them in the laboratory of my experience. Over that time, I have become happier and happier. Now it's your turn. What you are about to read works.

My fondest hope is that this book serves as a turning point in your own quest for happiness, and that these ideas bring as much comfort to your life as they have to mine and those of the countless others who have preceded you on this path. May they prove a trusty guide in your own pursuit of happiness, success and wellbeing.

With love,

Michael

ACKNOWLEDGEMENTS

And now ... have you ever seen one of those awards ceremonies where the winner tries to list in two minutes or less every single person who has contributed to their success?

My heartfelt thanks and appreciation go to:

Bill Cumming, Mandy Evans, Dr Richard Bandler and Paul McKenna, PhD – I shudder to think what my life would have been like if you had not become a part of it!

Alcinoo Giandinoto, Kerri Glass and Jessica Abiva, who have kept my business (and life) moving forward whenever I needed to take a step back

All the readers of the MNCT and members of the Genius Catalyst community who have supported me and my work over the past seven years

Jane Acton, Sue Crowley, Dotti Irving and Robert Kirby for their determination and persistence in getting my voice out into the world

My wonderful editor, Lizzie Hutchins, who understands that a real argument is not a dispute to be settled but a work of art to be evolved

The incredible staff at Hay House, in particular Michelle Pilley and Reid Tracy, whose unwavering belief in me is one of the most incredible gifts in my life.

The people on this list are special and their contribution to this book has been tremendous. It includes the giants on whose practical and philosophical shoulders I stand, as well as the teachers, mentors, coaches and friends who have supported me along the way.

Oli Barry	*Sophie Keller*
David Beeler	*Nancy Kline*
Steve Chandler	*Tom Konkle*
Michele Lisenbury Christensen	*John LaValle*
Larry Crane	*Jennifer Louden*
Dr John F. DeMartini	*Robert Mintz, PhD*
Bruce Di Marsico	*Dr James Pawelski*
Robert Dilts	*Jay Perry*
Ray Dodd	*Candace Pert, PhD*
Hale Dwoskin	*Lynn Robinson*
Peter Fenner	*Dr Ronald A. Ruden*
Gay and Kathlyn Hendricks	*Dr Martin Seligman*
Barry Neil Kaufman	*Clare Staples*
Byron Katie	*Win Wenger, PhD*

Finally, to my patient and supportive family, Nina, Oliver, Clara and Maisy – I can come out and play now. May you always know how incredibly much you are loved!

INTRODUCTION

*'I am by calling a dealer in words – and words are, of
course, the most powerful drug used by mankind.'*
Rudyard Kipling

This is a book about unreasonable happiness. It is about your
ability to feel happy not only when you get a promotion, win
the lottery and fall in love with the man or woman of your
dreams, but also when you lose your job, can't pay the
mortgage and are surrounded by screaming children.

It's about your ability to experience good feelings in your
body even when good things aren't happening in your life.
It's also about why feeling good when things are bad is one of
the fastest ways to make them change for the better.

The purpose of this book is for you to become happier –
to feel more of your good feelings and be more comfortable
with the bad ones. Over the course of the next few hours (or
days, or weeks, or however long you take to read the book
and experiment with the experiments), you will learn that
you are far more in control of your own wellbeing than you
ever thought possible. You will learn to make small changes in
the way you feel, think and act, and you will come to realize
that these small changes can make a big (actually, huge)
difference.

That's not to say that if you are angry, stressed out, anxious or depressed you can or should just 'pull yourself together and get on with it'. Life is often difficult, and blaming yourself for feeling bad is like trying to teach a pig to sing – it rarely works, and it tends to annoy the pig.

But if you want to have more choices about what you feel when, I'll be sharing the fruits of over 20 years of exploration into the structure of happiness and how you can use that understanding to feel good, feel better and even feel happy about whatever is happening in your life right now.

How this all works

My wife once asked me to define the difference between a therapist, a consultant and a coach. I referred to my trusted dictionary and was told that a therapist is someone who:

> *'...treats mental, physical, or psychological disorders by mental, physical, or psychological means.'*

A consultant, on the other hand, is:

> *'a person who provides expert advice professionally,'*

whereas the standard British definition of a coach is:

> *'a single-decker vehicle, especially one that is comfortably equipped and used for longer journeys.'*

(Which is nothing compared to the Australian definition of a coach as 'a docile cow or bullock used as a decoy to attract wild cattle'...)

My own definition of these three 'helping professionals' is a bit simpler – a therapist fixes what's broken, a consultant tells you what to do, and a coach, like the aforementioned single-decker vehicle, is comfortably equipped and trained to help you get wherever you want to go.

When my wife went on to ask me which one I was, I thought long and hard before realizing that while I inevitably did a little bit of all of those things, the heart of my approach didn't really fit any of them. What I am, and the role I hope to play with you throughout this book, is a *catalyst*.

Catalyst (n)
1. *An agent or substance that initiates or accelerates the rate of a reaction without being consumed in the process.*
2. *One that precipitates a process or event, especially without being directly involved in or changed by the consequences.*
3. *Someone or something that causes an important event to happen.*

Much of my background and psychological training is in a field called neuro-linguistic programming (NLP) – the study of how language impacts our neurology and behaviour. Since what I want is for you to be truly, deeply happy, in order to initiate and accelerate that process I have written this book using specific (and sometimes unusual) language patterns that will actually trigger chemical changes on the inside of your brain. You may begin to experience good feelings in your body and a greater sense of what's possible in your mind just by reading these words.

There are essentially two ways to read this book (or indeed any book that purports to tell you how to live more happily in the world): you can believe the book has all the answers or you can believe that you do.

I believe in you.

Over the past 16 years I've worked with over 10,000 people from all around the world, helping them to become happier and to live more and more wonderful lives. Some of these people are amongst the wealthiest and most successful in the world, while others are 'just plain folk' who simply want more out of life than a daily grind and a nightly battle with their own dark thoughts and unfulfilled dreams.

The reason I can work as effectively with a TV star, a CEO, a scientist and a housewife all in the same day is that I know something about each one of them which is also true of you:

You already have everything you need inside you to feel happy and live a meaningful life – the only question is access!

I've deliberately put more experiments in this book than anyone is likely to complete. That's so you can do the ones that capture your imagination and leave the rest for another time. Each experiment is designed to give you a tangible experience of your incredible capacity to choose and to change.

And if you choose to make this book about you and your happiness, you are about to embark on an adventure that will change your life for good.

The choice to feel happy

No matter how many times I talk about the benefits of feeling happy to individual clients or groups, the initial responses are the same:

'How can I feel happy? You clearly know nothing about my life!'

'Isn't it bad to feel happy when there's so much suffering in the world?'

'I wouldn't want to feel happy all the time.'

Or my personal favourite:

'You can't make me feel happy, you stupid American git!'

(Actually, most people are far too polite to actually say that last one to my face, but usually they're shouting it so loudly inside their heads that I manage to hear it anyway!)

While we'll take a closer look at each of these points in our very first chapter together, let me take a few moments here to address them *en masse*:

You are under no obligation to feel happy. Not feeling happy does not make you a bad person and I don't think you 'should' feel happy now or later or even all the time.

But what I do want you to know is that it is possible for you to feel happy – and that choice is yours to make at any moment.

The benefits of making that choice are both simple and profound:

1. It feels good

At the risk of beginning by stating the obvious, our bodies have a natural predisposition towards pleasure (good feelings) and away from pain (bad feelings). This is a biological survival instinct, and is governed by our limbic system and brain stem, which are the oldest parts of our brain. Given the choice between a perceived pain and a perceived pleasure, your brain will take you towards the pleasure and away from the pain every single time.

2. It makes you healthier

When 'happy chemicals' are released into your body, your

muscles relax and all your neurological and physiological systems return to their natural state. As most diseases can be traced at least partially to dis-ease in the body, this 'return to ease' that accompanies happiness is both comforting at the time and healing over the long term. In addition, a focus on care and compassion increases your body's production of IgA, a chemical which has an immediate positive impact on your immune system.

3. It makes you younger

A study by the Institute of HeartMath has shown that the simple act of visualizing someone you love while focusing your attention on your physical heart will increase your body's production of DHEA, the anti-ageing hormone. In addition, the positive effects of that little bit of good feeling will last in your body for up to seven hours. So not only can feeling happy help you to heal, it also acts as a sort of a 'spiritual Botox' for your body, making your skin softer, your eyes brighter and your entire appearance younger.

4. It makes you smarter

If you've ever struggled to solve a problem, you may have had the experience of being distracted from the struggle by the beauty of a sunset, a well-timed piece of gallows humour or even the sheer relief of giving up for a time. In the space that followed that interruption, you suddenly knew exactly what to do next.

This process is wonderfully described in Guy Claxton's book *Hare Brain, Tortoise Mind* as 'the triumph of wisdom over intellect' – and being able to access your inner wisdom 'on demand' will make you smarter than another 14 years of school ever could. (As a point of interest, it will also let you take full advantage of everything you learned in the first 14 years.)

5. *It makes you more successful*

Much of my first book was based on a simple premise:

> *Happiness leads to success a lot more often*
> *than success leads to happiness.*

The clarity of thought and easy flow of inspiration and intuition that accompany good feelings in your body make it easier to make the choices that lead to success. They also make success fun.

So in all these ways and more it turns out that happiness is not only a choice – it's an extremely practical choice, one that will not only make your life more pleasant, it will make it tangibly better, creating an optimal environment within which you can grow and prosper.

Happy matters

A venture capitalist I know who has had a great deal of success in his life is what I would call an 'open-minded sceptic' when it comes to anything that smacks of self-help or personal development. His first inclination is to dismiss any new idea as 'too simple', 'too stupid' or 'OK for other people', yet he's also oddly willing to give these things a try. (I suspect so that he can then reject them from first-hand experience!)

After the success of my first book, *You Can Have What You Want*, he asked me what my follow-up would be. When I told him that it was about how to feel happy, he seemed genuinely disappointed.

'Oh,' he said. 'It's going to be one of *those* books.'

I'm not sure exactly what he meant, but I asked him to try a little experiment. I asked him to think about a problem he was having – a situation in his life that he was feeling slightly overwhelmed by. When I noticed his eyes move down and his skin go a bit pale, I shouted 'Boo!' at him and he looked back up at me, startled but bemused.

Next I asked him to think a happy thought – to think about someone or something that made him smile. He seemed to find that a little bit harder, but he closed his eyes and when I saw a smile playing on his lips and the colour returning to his face, I guided him through the basic 'recipe for feeling good' exercise I will share with you in Chapter Three. Soon he was breathing deeply and evenly, his shoulders had relaxed and he had an expression of calm and peace on his face.

'Now,' I said to him, 'continuing to enjoy *these* feelings of ease and wellbeing, I want you to once again think about that situation you found overwhelming.'

As I said the word 'these', I reached over and gently squeezed his shoulder, creating a simple association between that touch and his good feelings.

I watched his face as he began to think about that old situation in a brand-new way. The muscles around his eyes tensed, then relaxed, then tense again, then relaxed even more.

When he seemed completely at peace, I told him to open his eyes and asked him what had happened.

'That was weird,' he said. 'When you asked me to think about a problem, I was going to think about something at work and then an image of my teenage daughter just popped into my head. We've been battling over pretty much everything for a while now and I was just getting back into our most recent argument when you startled me.'

He looked at me with a strange smile on his face.

'Then, when you asked me to think a happy thought, I thought about my daughter again, but this time it was when she was a little girl. God, she could make me laugh! At first I was just playing along with you, but it really did feel good to think about that, so I gave myself over to the good feelings and just decided to enjoy it.

'When you squeezed my shoulder and asked me to think about the problems I'd been having with my daughter again, it was really confusing – like I couldn't quite remember what it was about it that I had been finding so difficult.'

I then asked him, 'So what's changed about your relationship with your daughter just from having taken a few minutes out to feel happy before thinking about it again?'

His analytical mind kicked back in and he said, somewhat dismissively, 'Well obviously, nothing's changed!'

Within a few moments, the smile returned to his eyes as he said somewhat reflectively, 'But everything's different.'

And this to me is the whole point of happiness (if indeed feeling happy needs 'a point'):

When you're happy, nothing changes – but everything is different.

'Mental mountains' are reduced into molehills; problems that seemed insoluble begin to dissolve in the light of your happy awareness. If there are things for you to do in order to make things more the way you want them to be, you have a remarkable sense of clarity about what to do and a remarkable sense of ease about doing it. In other words, your life may not look any different on the outside, but it feels completely different on the inside. And those new feelings of happiness are often the only difference you need to make all the difference in the world.

So if you're ready to feel happy now – even if you're not quite sure that it's really possible for you – let's get things started...

PART I

Feeling Good

Chapter One

GETTING STARTED

The three myths of happiness

'Myths which are believed in tend to become true.'
George Orwell

There are over 60,000 books in print at the moment on the subject of happiness, which is particularly interesting when you consider the fact that 'happiness' doesn't even exist.

Like 'success', 'love' and 'confidence' (not to mention 'stress', 'anxiety' and 'depression'), the word 'happiness' is what linguists call a 'nominalization' – a process or activity that is described as if it were a tangible thing.

While the metaphor of happiness as a 'thing' does make it easier to talk about, it also carries with it some interesting baggage.

If happiness were a thing:

- *It could be lost or found outside yourself.*
- *You could give it to or get it from someone else.*
- *You could almost certainly buy it (and it would be cheaper and quicker to get on the Internet).*
- *You could share it with others.*

This, of course, fits with the way that many of us think about happiness. But if our goal is to actually feel happy not only now but more and more of the time, it is useful to think about 'happiness' in terms of a process:

> **Happiness is the process of creating and experiencing good feelings in your body and mind, moment by moment by moment.**

When you recognize happiness as a process, not a thing, you realize:

- *You can do it or not do it.*
- *You can get better at it.*
- *You can ultimately master it.*

Over 400 years ago Francis Bacon wrote about what he called 'the idols of the Western world' – those ideas that were so much a part of our culture that we never thought to question them, instead worshipping them with the kind of blind faith normally reserved for religious rather than scientific pursuits.

I prefer to think of these ideas as myths – stories we tell ourselves about how the world works that are blindly passed on from generation to generation and never questioned until the moment we decide to value our own experience over and above the ideas before our minds.

Myth number one: *'I'll be happy when...'*

People tend to think that happiness is just around the corner and will miraculously arrive the moment they get their act together, achieve all their goals, find the man or woman of their dreams and attain spiritual enlightenment. But is it really true?

Have you ever reached a goal or got something you always wanted, only to find that within a few months, weeks or even moments, the thrill was gone and you were back searching for that elusive something which would fill the hole and fulfil your longing for something greater?

If all there were to happiness was getting what you wanted, the richest and most outwardly successful people in our society would be the happiest. But it only takes a quick glance through the pages of today's newspapers before you are reading about the latest miserable millionaire or celebrity scandal.

The reality is simply this:

> *Your happiness does not depend*
> *on getting or having what you want.*

When we step out from behind the myth and become willing to pursue happiness directly, we also become free to move happily forward in the direction of our goals and dreams.

Myth number two: *It's not possible to be happy in certain situations*

The idea that our happiness and wellbeing in life are the product of our circumstances seems at first glance to be self-evident. After all, isn't everybody sad at a funeral? And when's the last time you saw a group of football fans celebrating after their team lost a big game?

But in the same way that the regular presence of fire engines at the scene of a fire doesn't mean that fire engines cause fires, the regular presence of unhappiness in certain situations doesn't mean the situation caused the unhappiness.

The truth behind this myth is a subtle one:

> *While it may or may not be possible to be happy all the time, it is certainly possible to be happy at any time.*

In fact, each one of those situations you think of as 'making' you unhappy is simply an area of your life in which you think that it would be inappropriate to feel happy (for example at a funeral) or that feeling happy would be in some way bad for you.

(Don't worry if that doesn't make sense to you just yet – we'll be talking more about it a little later!)

Myth number three: *Unhappiness is good for us*

It is undeniable that unhappiness is a part of life, and many philosophers and scientists point to the evolutionary role that fear and anger have played in the survival of the species. But when we start to justify our bad feelings as being good for us (or, worse still, our good feelings as being bad for us), we keep ourselves stuck in a self-fulfilling rut.

Ironically, the state of discomfort most of us put ourselves into to better deal with our problems is the worst possible state in which to deal with them. Like pouring fuel on a fire, meeting difficulties with anger, fear and sadness tends to make things more, well, difficult.

Here's what's waiting for us on the other side of this myth:

> *Whatever you can do with unhappiness you can do better when you're happy.*

As long as we justify our unhappiness as being necessary and important, we'll make sure that we have more of it. The moment we recognize that our chief aims in life are almost entirely achievable with positive emotion, we can change the very basis of our lives.

The happy formula

There are three main things you need to learn and practise in order to feel happy not only now but whenever you want for the rest of your life:

1. Give yourself better feelings.
2. Tell yourself better stories.
3. Act on your inner knowing.

These three steps make up what I call 'the happy formula' and correspond to the three areas of happiness spoken about in ancient and modern philosophy – emotional happiness (feelings), judgemental happiness (stories) and moral happiness (right action). As you learn to feel, think and act happily in the world, you will find that each skill builds on the one before, ultimately forming a wonderfully happy circle:

> *The better you feel, the better stories you tend to tell yourself about your life.*
>
> *The better stories you tell yourself about your life, the easier it is to do what you know is right for you.*
>
> *The more you do what you know is right for you, the better you feel.*

In other words, the better you feel in your body, the easier it is to practise the skills that create the internal and external environments which foster happiness. And practice works for any of us, no matter where or when we start.

The stupid thumb

When I was a child, there was a rumour going around the

school yard that depending on which thumb was on top when you folded your hands with interlacing fingers, it meant you were stupid.

While I no longer remember which one it was, I was horrified to discover that I had the 'stupid' thumb. I immediately made plans to pack up all my worldly belongings into a small shopping bag and head for the hills where people with all kinds of thumbs could live together in peace and harmony. However, after a long and heartfelt talk with my favourite stuffed animal, I decided that rather than run away I would face up to my demons and force my thumbs to behave like the intelligent digits I knew them to be.

I embarked on a programme of conditioning my body to behave in a new way. Each morning I would consciously interlace my fingers at least 100 times, being sure to place the 'non-stupid' thumb on top. At first, it felt incredibly odd to connect my hands in the 'wrong' way. But after only a few mornings it began to feel more and more normal. At some point in the first two weeks I closed my eyes and brought my hands together. When I opened my eyes, the new thumb was on top.

I had done it – I had changed what felt 'normal' and 'comfortable' simply by consciously repeating a new behaviour on a regular basis. And despite the fact that I now recognize that the only thing it had to do with my level of intelligence was that I believed it, I did learn an important lesson in the process:

You become what you practise.

Whatever we do consistently (i.e. practise), we get better at. If we practise anger, we get better at being angry. If we practise shutting down our emotions, we get better at feeling depressed. And if we practise giving ourselves better feelings, telling ourselves better stories and acting on our inner knowing, we will get better and better at feeling happy.

The question is, what are you practising now?

Chapter Two

THE ART AND SCIENCE OF DELIGHT

How to feel sad

*'The first and simplest emotion which we discover
in the human mind is curiosity.'*
Edmund Burke

One day, when my son was six, I walked into his bedroom to
find him all teary-eyed, snuggled up in the arms of a giant
teddy bear named Harvey. When I asked him why he was so
sad, he said, 'I was thinking about my friend Thomas and how
we're not really friends any more because he's mean to me.'

While I was tempted to interrupt and congratulate my
son for setting strong boundaries at such a tender age, I bit
my tongue and asked, 'Is that why you're sad?'

'No,' he replied, seeming genuinely surprised at the
thought. 'I'm sad because if I think really, really hard about
how much fun we could have been having if we were still
friends, it makes me cry.'

Tears in my eyes, I had to agree with him that that was
indeed an excellent way to make yourself sad.

Truth is, I can remember the day he first figured out how
to make himself feel sad. One night our cat, Mason, was run
over outside our house in London. The next morning, my
then three-year-old son was excitedly telling everybody all
about the gross thing that had happened to his cat. By the

end of the day, having successfully gauged the reactions of the grown-ups around him, he had learned to tell the story in a 'sad voice' and act it out with pursed lips, hunched shoulders and lowered eyes.

So, if you want to feel sad, here's a simple three-step recipe:

1. Think really, really hard about things that make you sad.
2. Talk about those things in a 'sad voice'.
3. Purse your lips (you can cry if you want), hunch your shoulders and lower your eyes.

Why this works so well is easy to understand if you take a closer look at how we create our personal experience of any given moment. There are essentially three variables which comprise the structure of our subjective experience:

1. The way we use our body.
2. The maps we make in our head.
3. The stories we tell ourselves.

This model was first developed by Dr Richard Bandler in the field of neuro-linguistic programming (NLP) and it can be used to make sense of how we create all our experiences. Let's take a closer look at each of these three elements:

1. The way we use our body

An exercise I used to do at the beginning of my trainings was to ask each person in the group to stand up tall, look up towards the ceiling, put a big toothy grin on their face – and feel depressed!

No matter how long they stood there, if they continued standing up straight and tall, eyes up, with an embarrassingly silly, toothy grin on their faces, they found themselves utterly unable to depress themselves. (Though they were often capable of making themselves extremely angry with me afterwards for asking them to do something quite so silly!)

You can test the connection between how you use your body and how you feel inside right now.

> Go ahead and sit the way you would be sitting if reading this book were the most boring thing you've ever had to do. (Hopefully, you shifted your body in some way to do it – if not, stop reading immediately and go get yourself a different book!)
>
> Now move so that you are sitting the way you would be sitting if you were curious about what I was about to say, in the way that you might be curious about what was inside your presents on your birthday...
>
> Finally, shift your body until you are sitting the way you would be sitting if you knew that the very next thing I will tell you in this chapter is the key to a lifetime of happiness and will also enable you to achieve all your most important goals and single-handedly bring about world peace...
>
> Got it?
>
> Good.
>
> Now stay that way as you read through the rest of this book!

While I'm obviously not expecting you to actually do this, it's interesting to think about how much more enjoyable your experience might be if you decide to give it a try...

2. The maps we make in our head

In order to make sense of the world, we re-present the information we take in through our five senses inside our mind – that is, we make an internal representation of the information, sort of like an inner map. We then make decisions and choose our actions based on those inner maps.

Of course, in order to make a map you need to leave things out (otherwise the map would be as large as the territory), make generalizations (all water is blue, all parks are green etc.) and distort perspectives to make everything fit. This is what makes a map useful, but it is also what creates problems.

Here's the key:

What we perceive to be problems in our lives are nothing to do with what is happening in the world and everything to do with the limitations of our mental maps.

When you understand this, you can understand how changing your mind (i.e. your map) can literally change your life.

If a picture is worth 1,000 words, take a look at this one...

Think of a (small) problem you've been having. It can be one you've been dealing with for a long time or a brand-new one. (I love brand-new problems – they're so shiny!) Notice where in space you represent the problem. If you're not sure, just point to where you think it might be.

Next, notice if you're looking at the problem through your own eyes or if you can see yourself in the image. Is it moving or still? Clear or fuzzy? Large or small?

Now, take the problem picture and if you were looking

through your own eyes, step out of it so that you can see yourself in it. Push the picture a comfortable distance away. If it was moving (like a film), make it still (like a photograph). If it was clear, make it fuzzy. If it was large, shrink it down until it's the size of a postage stamp. Then stick it on an envelope and post it to someone you think can handle it. I'll wait…

Now think about the 'problem' again. For most of you, it won't feel as significant as it did before you began. If it does, continue to play with the details of your representation until you've given yourself a new perspective.

3. The stories we tell ourselves

The third structure we use to create our subjective experience is language. Language is another mapping tool – one we use to create, describe and share our experiences with one another. We do this primarily by telling ourselves (and others) stories about what we have experienced.

In a recent cover story from *New Scientist* magazine, Helen Phillips wrote:

> 'There is certainly plenty of evidence that much of what we do is the result of unconscious brain processing, and that our consciousness seems to be interpreting what has happened, rather than driving it….
>
> Our senses may take in more than 11 million pieces of information each second, whereas even the most liberal estimates suggest that we are conscious of just 40 of these….
>
> It is an unsettling thought that perhaps all our conscious mind ever does is dream up stories in an attempt to make sense of our world.'

This new research supports the idea that it is our unconscious minds that drive most of our decisions and behaviour. Even our memories aren't really real, but rather maps and stories that we have constructed with internal images, sounds and feelings in order to 'make sense' of our experience.

Together, all of these elements – the way we use our body, the way we make our internal maps and the stories we tell ourselves about why and how we're doing it – create our neuro-physiological state.

Since feeling good is a particularly useful (and pleasant) neuro-physiological state, it is worth learning to adapt your physiology, representations and stories to create this state inside you.

Take a moment now to do this for yourself...

Creating a good feeling

1. Notice how you're feeling in your body right now.
2. Shift your body until you're feeling just a little bit better. You could do this by sitting up straighter or getting up and giving yourself a gentle stretch, smiling up into your eyes and down into your body, or simply taking a deep breath and feeling it spread into every part of yourself.
3. Next, talk to yourself in a friendly voice. Tell yourself something you genuinely want to hear. Offer yourself a sincere compliment or remember a time where you received a compliment and you knew it was sincere. Enjoy the good feelings that come with receiving that sincere compliment.
4. Make a picture of yourself in your mind as you would look if you were just a little bit happier than you are right now. When you've got it, step into the picture and enjoy the good feelings.
5. Repeat each of the steps above until you have successfully created a smile on your face and a good feeling in your body!

In order to better understand why this technique works so well, let's explore a little bit of the science behind it...

The chemistry of happiness

> 'Everything should be made as simple as
> possible – but no simpler.'
> Albert Einstein

According to the latest research into the science of emotion, every feeling we have in our body is a 'neuro-chemical event'. That is, every time we perceive something in the world and then interpret it in our brains, certain chemicals are released into our bodies. When everything is working perfectly, just the right amounts of just the right chemicals are released to put our bodies into an optimal state for whatever action is required.

For example, if you were to walk out of your cave one morning and encounter an angry woolly mammoth on the way to work, your brain would no doubt interpret this as a danger and trigger the release of adrenaline and cortisol into your body. These chemicals would cause you to narrow your focus, sharpen your thinking, empty your bowels, temporarily increase your strength (like Popeye's spinach!) and prepare you to either fight the mammoth or run like hell in the opposite direction.

When it comes to happiness, there are two different chemicals we're interested in:

a. Dopamine

Dopamine is the 'motivation chemical'. The release of dopamine into the bloodstream increases our ability to focus and motivates us to take action. Dopamine levels naturally rise as we move towards a goal and begin to anticipate a result. They tend to be at their highest when we are in active pursuit of getting our most basic needs met.

b. Serotonin

Serotonin is the 'feel-good chemical' and is as calming and soothing as dopamine is energizing. When dopamine produces effort, serotonin provides the reward.

We receive an increase in serotonin whenever we:

- *Win anything, from a game of noughts and crosses to the National Lottery.*
- *Get public recognition for a job well done.*
- *Take certain drugs or drink alcohol.*
- *Feel part of a crowd, group or team (for example at a football match or a book club).*

Together, the interplay of dopamine and serotonin make the world go round. Higher levels of dopamine move us forward; higher levels of serotonin provide feelings of safety, satisfaction and curiosity.

When looked at through this chemical filter, we can understand the innate appeal of goal-driven behaviour, whether it's trying to do a Sudoku puzzle or change the world. We not only get the energized, focused sensations that come from the build-up of dopamine in trying to solve the puzzle or reach the goal; we also get the calm, contented feelings of satisfaction and wellbeing that follow the release of serotonin at the moment of triumph and success.

We can also understand why it's so imperative to get our brain chemistry firing on all cylinders. One recent study showed that in autopsies of over 63 people who had committed suicide over the course of a year, a common factor was a complete lack of serotonin in the bloodstream.

In other words, when the serotonin goes, the will to live can go with it. But when you fill your brain with happy chemicals, you feel good in your body now and optimistic about the future.

While there are certain pharmaceutical drugs and natural remedies which have been shown to increase the body's stores of serotonin (and others which block and limit it), they lie outside of the scope of this book. Instead, we are interested in how we can release 'happy chemicals' into our bloodstream on demand, using nothing more than our understanding, attention and intention.

And in order to do that, we need to take a look at a third chemical, closely linked to serotonin but with some wonderfully unique properties all its own...

The nectar of the gods

'You would then reach into your bag and pull out a Fuzzy the size of a child's hand. As soon as the Fuzzy saw the light of day it would smile and blossom into a large, shaggy, Warm Fuzzy. When you laid the Warm Fuzzy on the person's head, shoulder or lap it would snuggle up and melt right against their skin and make them feel good all over.'

From *A Warm Fuzzy Tale* by Claude M. Steiner

In the early 1970s, a graduate student named Candace Pert discovered that every cell in our body contained what she called 'opiate receptors'. She found these receptors were particularly in tune with one special kind of chemical messenger called 'endogenous morphines', more commonly known as 'endorphins'. Endorphins (or, as my four-year-old calls them, 'en-dolphins') are your body's natural opiates, the neurotransmitters that control pain and create pleasure. They are the biochemical source of that happy, glowing feeling that Claude Steiner calls 'the Warm Fuzzy'.

Whenever you feel a warm glow after sex, the sweet feeling of looking at an extremely cute puppy or baby, or even the release and relaxation of climbing into a warm bath at the end of a hard day, what you're feeling is endorphins swimming happily through your bloodstream.

You get a natural endorphin release when you do physical exercise, make love, laugh a lot and relax deeply. And not only does the presence of endorphins in your system make you feel better, but it can make you smarter and more capable as well. As Paul McKenna says in his book *Change Your Life in Seven Days*:

> *'Because endorphins are neuro-transmitters, they create more bonding in the brain, so every time you experience an endorphin release, they actually make you more intelligent. And every cell in your body has receptors for endorphins. How great a design feature is that? Not only can every cell in our body experience happiness, but the more often we choose to be happy, the more intelligent we become!*
>
> *The best thing about understanding the phenomenal role of endorphins in our health, happiness and wellbeing is that we don't have to wait for spontaneous releases of endorphins in order to experience their benefits – we can cultivate the endorphin response through practice.'*

Let's do a quick experiment so you can experience this for yourself:

Imagine your body is filled with golden light. (It can actually be whatever colour you like – any colour that brings a smile to your face when you think about it.)

Now imagine that light flowing throughout your body like a warm liquid, nourishing every cell and organ along the way.

If you look closely, you can see tiny little 'en-dolphins' swimming in the light. Each en-dolphin is a carrier of joy.

Imagine yourself diving into the light and swimming with the en-dolphins. You can continue doing this for as long as it feels good...

Soon, you will find that just thinking about swimming with your own endorphins will bring a wave of good feelings to your body and mind! The more you practise, the easier it becomes.

A measure of happiness

In order to better evaluate the benefits of this 'happy practice' over time, I'd like to propose the use of an extremely simple measure – what researchers call a 'subjective happiness scale':

How happy are you feeling at the moment on a scale from 1 to 10, where 1 is the most horrible feeling you can imagine and 10 is the most wonderful feeling you can imagine?

Don't worry about what the number is or how it might compare to the numbers of the people around you – we'll only be using this scale to compare you to you.

Now, answer this question:

What could you do right now to take yourself up the 'subjective happiness scale' by 1 – that is, from a 3 to a 4 or an 8 to a 9?

Have a quick think and then do whatever it is – you can carry on reading when you've bumped yourself at least one number up the scale...

What did you do?

Did you take a deep breath and smile? Think a happy thought? Think about someone you love or someone (or something) who loves you?

Perhaps you got up and stretched or jotted down a quick note to get something out of your head so you could be fully present to what you're reading now.

If you got stuck (or just skipped ahead without playing along!), try this instead:

Take yourself down the subjective happiness scale by one – from a 10 to a 9, a 7 to a 6, or even a 2 to a 1. I'll wait....

What did you do?

Did you think about something you'd been worrying about and hadn't been able to get out of your head? Did you make pictures of bad things happening to people that you cared about or tell yourself scary stories about something that might not work out in your favour? (Or, worse still, how crap you are at exercises like this?)

OK, one last experiment...

Imagine what it would be like to live your life from an 8, 9 or 10. Really step into your imagination and think about being truly, deeply happy in the kinds of situations you normally find yourself in at work, with friends and at home. Imagine feeling the way you feel when things are really wonderful.

Would people notice? Would they wonder what had happened to you?

If you did nothing else in this book, just practising releasing your own endorphins and feeling good on a regular basis would make a tremendous difference to the quality of your life. And, as you've probably begun to experience, creating feelings of happiness in your body is surprisingly simple to do. What can be more difficult is allowing those happy feelings to permeate your life.

We'll take a look at why that is and what you can do about it in our very next chapter...

Chapter Three

HAPPINESS RULES

The permission principle

> *'Most people are about as happy as they
> make their minds up to be.'*
> Abraham Lincoln

When would 'now' be a good time to feel happy?

Contrary to what you may think, the number-one obstacle to your feeling happy now is not your job, your boyfriend, the weather, the time of the month or even the state of the economy. It is your own willingness to feel happy in spite of all these things.

To put it another way, the reason you are not feeling happy now (if indeed you are not feeling happy now) is simply because at some level, it's not OK with you to feel happy until you've sorted out:

- *your moods*
- *your bank balance*
- *your relationship(s)*
- *your clutter*
- *your weight*
- *your 'bad' habits*
- *your life.*

This is what I call 'the permission principle':

You will feel happy in direct proportion to your willingness to feel happy without anything in your life changing from how it is right now.

The reason more people aren't happier more of the time isn't because they couldn't be – it's because they think they shouldn't be. And if you don't think it's OK for you to feel happy right now, it isn't all that likely that you will.

What you're up against is that voice inside your head which goes a little something like this:

'It's not OK for me to feel happy now because something in my life is not quite right (although I'm not necessarily sure exactly what that is). I need to stay unsettled and at least slightly uncomfortable until I've dealt with whatever it is that's not quite right – to stay in a state of heightened awareness to remind myself that there's something I needto deal with in the future.'

The problem is, our definition of 'not quite right' is almost unfathomably broad.

Why are you unhappy?

In her book *Composing a Life*, Mary Catherine Bateson shares the story of a conversation she had as a young child with her father, the famous social anthropologist Gregory Bateson.

According to Mary Catherine, she was unhappy about how everything on her desk was always messed up. Her father asked her how she knew it was 'messed up' and she responded by explaining that her ruler was not in a straight line parallel to her blotter, which was not equidistant from the corners of her desk. And don't even get her started about the arrangement and relative sharpness of her pencils!

After several minutes of this, her father replied, 'The reason everything always seems to be so messed up is because there is only one way for things to be right, but over 1,000 ways they can be messed up.'

And most of us have designed our lives in the exact same way. We have thousands upon thousands of ways our lives can be messed up, the vast majority of which are completely outside our control. This puts us firmly at the mercy of circumstance in a world where most people's circumstances aren't really known for being merciful. Consequently, we only give ourselves permission to feel truly happy in those all-too-rare moments when the fates align and all our conditions for happiness are mysteriously (and temporarily) met.

How specifically do you know when it's OK (or not OK) to feel happy now? By consulting the 'rule book' in your head – and since you didn't consciously choose most of these rules, you may find they begin to change as they come up into your conscious awareness.

Let's take a look at a few of them right now...

1. Make a list of situations in which you think it would be uncomfortable, inappropriate or 'just plain wrong' to feel happy; for example:

   - *a funeral*
   - *after losing a big game*
   - *when your partner is mad at you.*

2. Now make a list of 'approved' situations when feeling happy 'makes sense'; for example:

   - *a wedding*
   - *after winning a big game*
   - *when your partner is happy with you.*

3. For each of the 'just plain wrong' situations, ask yourself the following questions:

   Why would it be wrong to feel happy in this situation?

   What am I concerned it would mean about me if I felt happy in this situation?

   What am I afraid I would or wouldn't do if I felt happy in this situation?

Once you recognize the role permission plays in your pursuit of happiness, you will see that there are really three questions you need to answer before you can fully engage in the process of becoming 'unreasonably happy':

- *Do I want to feel happy now?*
- *Am I willing to feel happy now?*
- *How can I feel happy now?*

Without first taking the time to answer the first two questions, there's almost no point in answering the third. With the exception of extreme depression and anxiety, feeling happy is more often a question of 'will' or 'won't' than 'can' or 'can't'.

Over the next few pages I will be sharing with you a simple three-step process that will enable you to feel happy in your body regardless of what is going on in your world.

As you practise these techniques over time, you are retraining your nervous system to experience a fairly steady flow of endorphins through your body on an ongoing basis. The more you do this, the more good feelings you will be able to handle. What is now your 10 will become a 1 as you gain access to levels of bliss and wellbeing you may not yet be able to imagine.

Before long, you will begin to be 'overcome by good feelings' even when you haven't been consciously practising them – during a movie, while walking in the park, even in the middle of a crowded supermarket. And the more often you allow yourself to feel good, the better you get to feel.

A recipe for feeling good

In the same way that a recipe tells you exactly what you need to do to cook a meal but allows you a great deal of scope and sway in how you do it, I would now like to introduce you to a three-step recipe for happiness and wellbeing you can cook up in the midst of any circumstance or situation.

Here are the three steps in a nutshell:

1. Go to your heart and trigger a good feeling.
2. Crank up the intensity of the good feeling and spread it throughout your body.
3. Focus on the positive benefits of feeling this way both now and in the future.

Let's go through each of these in a bit more detail. If you like, you can actually do each step as you read about it now...

1. Go to your heart and trigger a good feeling

According to research done by the Institute of HeartMath, your emotional states are reflected in your heart rhythms. When you create greater coherence in your heart rhythms (by focusing your attention on your physical heart and awakening feelings of love and appreciation), your emotional states will follow suit.

Specifically, what I'd like you to do is this:

Put at least one hand on your chest above your physical heart. Now take three slow and gentle breaths into your heart. Think about someone you love or someone who loves you until you begin to feel the release of endorphins – like a warm fuzzy feeling in the very centre of your chest…

2. Crank up the intensity of the good feeling and spread it throughout your body

Once you've triggered a good feeling, your next step is to turn it up and spread it throughout your body. There are many ways to do this, but here are a few of my favourites. Don't worry if they don't all work for you first time – just choose the one which seems best for now and go for it!

a. Picture the good feeling in your heart as your favourite colour. The more vividly you see the colour, the better the feeling gets. Visualize the colour like a bucket of paint dripping throughout your entire body from the top of your head all the way down to the tips of your toes.

b. Imagine the good feeling in your heart is like a warm liquid or golden honey. Experiment until you find just the right temperature inside. Then taste and feel the warm honey-like liquid as it spreads throughout every cell of your body.

c. Experience the good feeling in your heart like a gentle tingling energy. Notice that you can speed up the tingling or slow it down until it feels absolutely wonderful. Now, direct this wonderful energy until you can feel your whole body tingling.

3. Focus on the positive benefits of feeling this way both now and in the future

In order to take full advantage of the good feeling that is hopefully dancing inside your body even now, you can decide that it's not only OK to feel happy now but that it will also be good for you in the future.

Here are a few simple ways to do this now:

> While bathing in the healing bliss of your own flow of endorphins, think about the fact that your nervous system is actively repairing itself and recovering from the stresses and strains of daily life.
>
> Rest in the awareness that each time you allow yourself to 'cook up' these good feelings inside your body, you are creating and strengthening neural pathways in your brain that are making it easier and more natural for you to feel happy in the future.
>
> Imagine how much easier the challenges of your life will be when you return to them having taken this time out to refresh your body and recharge your mind...

Happy practice

While in theory happiness makes us feel wonderful, in practice it enables us to create a more and more wonderful life. The three tools we use to build our happiness – the way we use our body, the maps we make in our minds and the stories we tell ourselves – are the same three tools we use to make ourselves miserable. Once you master the process, you get to choose the result.

Before long, you'll recognize something very important:

The only thing between you and feeling happy now
is a story.

In the next section of this book I'll be sharing with you some of the ways I've learned to not only reduce your uncomfortable feelings at any moment but also to build up reserves of positive feelings that will carry you through the most difficult of circumstances with ease and grace.

Until then, consider the story of the seeker who wanted to know more about being truly happy...

A master of happiness was travelling with a heavy bag upon his shoulder when he came across a seeker. The seeker asked him what true happiness really felt like.

The master paused for a moment, then smiled and took the bag off his shoulder. As it dropped heavily to the ground, he stood tall in the freedom from the heavy burden he had been carrying.

The seeker said, 'I think I understand. And what do you do once you're happy?'

The master smiled, picked up his bag and carried on down the road.

When you're ready to carry on down the road, I'll be waiting for you in the next chapter!

PART 2

Feeling Better

Chapter Four

WHAT'S YOUR STORY?

The facts of life

'I am a lover of what is, not because I am a spiritual person, but because it hurts when I argue with reality.'
Byron Katie

One morning I went outside and saw that some builders had dumped wet concrete on my lawn in the process of 'cleaning up' after a job. Big problem – the lawn was fairly newly seeded and the concrete had now mixed with the dirt and hardened. I was probably going to have to dig up the lawn and start again. My mind began to race as I considered the many things I would need to do to fix the problem and perhaps 'fix' the builders in the process.

In the midst of quietly and not so quietly fuming about it, I received a call from a client whose father was on his way to have an 'inoperable' brain tumour operated on by some surgeons who fortunately forgot to read the manual about what can't be done.

When I returned outside about 20 minutes later, I noticed with interest there was still some concrete on my lawn. What had changed is that it was no longer a problem – it had returned to just being concrete.

In order to make something into a 'problem', you have to do one of two things:

1. Compare it to how things used to be and decide they should be that way again, even though they're not.
2. Compare it to how you would like it to be and decide it should be that way now, even though it isn't.

In other words, in order to turn a fact of life into a problem to be solved, you first have to create a story about how things should be instead.

I remember when my parents dropped me off at the airport before I first moved to London at the age of 20. I was excited about the trip and couldn't wait to get on the plane. I was about to begin a new chapter in my life, the story of an actor striving to make his mark in the footsteps of Edmund Kean, Laurence Olivier and Albert Finney. It wasn't until I saw my parents' palpable sadness as they walked away from the departure gate that it occurred to me they too were beginning a new chapter, but their story was about an ageing couple whose last child was fleeing the nest. Same event, completely different experience.

The making of meaning

Our story is the meaning we give to the facts of our life – our interpretation of reality. If we make the facts of our life mean good things about us and the future, we will feel happy about them; if we make them mean bad things, we will feel unhappy about them. Either way, we're the ones making the meaning.

On my live trainings, I often do an exercise with participants where I invite them to come up with multiple meanings for a significant life event by repeatedly asking the question: 'What else could this mean?'

For example, if someone says their partner has left them, most people will assume that's a bad thing and will respond accordingly with a blend of sympathy and encouragement. But what else could it mean?

Here are some typical answers from seminar participants – you'll notice that some make it a good thing, some bad and some relatively neutral:

> *'Now they're free to meet someone who's* really *right for them.'*
>
> *'They'll never meet anyone else and they'll be alone – and miserable – for the rest of their lives.'*
>
> *'What they learn from the experience will make them a more loving partner in the future.'*
>
> *'They're scarred for life and will never experience love again.'*
>
> *'It's an opportunity to fight to win their partner back.'*
>
> *'It's life's way of saying "Time to move on."'*

After a few rounds of the game, it becomes clear that it's possible to make up hundreds of different meanings for any given event. The more optimistic the meaning, the better the accompanying feelings; the less optimistic, the worse the story feels.

But when you've played the game long enough a new, even more useful question emerges:

What do you want it to mean?

When you realize that you are literally making up the meaning of even the most significant 'facts' of your life, you can begin deliberately choosing the meanings which feel good and empower positive action. As I say to my clients:

If you're going to make stuff up,
make up good stuff.

The way to consistently 'make up good stuff' is to understand and master what cognitive psychologists call your 'explanatory style'.

In his research into pessimism, optimism, depression and happiness, Dr Martin Seligman noticed that people who tended to explain bad things as permanent, personal and pervasive had a completely different experience of life from those who explained their problems as being temporary and specific and didn't take them personally.

I had been teaching the idea of explanatory style for several years before I really experienced the full power of it for myself. One of my students was a medical doctor and I called him for advice the morning of a presentation I was due to make at Regent's College in London. My stomach ached, my head was killing me and I felt like I was going to die. Inside, I was telling myself a dramatic story about how I should have taken better care of myself (personal), and being sick meant I was an irresponsible person (pervasive). In addition, I could imagine myself throwing up during the presentation, being kicked out of the college and told never to darken their doors again (permanent).

When I asked the doctor what he thought I should do, he asked me a few diagnostic questions and then told me it sounded as though I had the 'three-hour flu', which apparently could strike anyone. If I was willing to ride it out, I would feel better within a few hours. In fact, I felt better the moment I got off the phone. Although I wasn't at my best, I got through the presentation with ease.

It was only afterwards, when I thought about what had happened, that I called my doctor friend back. When I questioned him about it, he somewhat sheepishly admitted he'd made up the three-hour flu diagnosis. He knew from my description of symptoms that I wasn't dangerously ill, but he also knew he couldn't make me well in the few minutes we had together over the phone.

He said he could tell I was making things worse with the scary stories I was telling myself, so he quickly reviewed our class notes while I was talking and made up an explanation for the bad feelings in my body which was impersonal, temporary and specific.

I'm not sure to this day which one of us was more surprised that it had actually worked!

Try this simple experiment in changing your 'explanatory style'. It's easiest to do this on paper but you can also do it aloud with a friend...

Why things are the way they are

1. Think of a situation in your life that went badly. Now answer the question 'Why did it go badly?' as if you were explaining it to a friend.
2. Once again explain why it went badly, but this time take out any reference to it being your fault in any way. (This is the first 'p': personalization.)
3. Now explain what happened again, but as if it were a one-off, one-time occurrence with a beginning, middle and end. (This is the second 'p': permanence.)
4. Finally, explain the situation as if it were an isolated downpoint in the otherwise awesome panorama of positivity that is your life! (This is the third 'p': pervasiveness.)
5. Notice which of the three changes (personalization, permanence, pervasiveness) made the biggest

> impact on your state and begin to rewrite the stories
> of your life from this new and different point of
> view.

The wonderful thing about being able to change the meanings of your life and your explanatory style is that your story begins to loosen its hold over your life. In fact, if I were going to nominate one key factor in both the success of my business and my marriage, it would be my recognition of the fact that my story is just a story and doesn't need to be given much weight. Therefore, while my default thinking about things can at times be quite pessimistic, it doesn't have the hold over my behaviour that it would if I really believed it.

Challenging your stories of impending doom is not only powerful, it's fun – and it serves as an ongoing reminder that no matter how detailed or practised your story is, it's still only a story. The question is, who's telling it?

Meeting the storyteller

Nearly everyone I have ever met or worked with experiences a voice or set of voices in their head that seems to have an opinion about everything that they do, don't do or even think about doing or not doing. (And if you think you don't have a voice inside your head, isn't it a voice inside your head telling you that?)

I call this collection of inner voices 'the storyteller'. Your inner storyteller is the narrator of your life, translating what you see and hear and feel into descriptions, assessments, judgements and observations. It began doing this at an early age, turning the facts of your life into stories to be told and problems to be solved.

Now if you listen very carefully, you may hear your mind trying to turn what I've just said into a problem – either by thinking you don't have a storyteller or that storytellers are bad and wrong. The part of your mind which is either agreeing with or questioning what I've just said is the storyteller in action!

Here are some ideas you can put into practice immediately that will help you create a more positive relationship with your inner storyteller:

1. Write it down

When I'm working on things which are outside my comfort zone, my inner storyteller kicks into overdrive. What I've noticed is that if I stay engaged in the process long enough, the storyteller goes quiet.

One day, just for fun, I decided to catalogue the many things that voice inside my head had to say about why I should give up on a project I was working on:

Variations on 'I want to quit' = 4

Variations on 'I can't do this' = 6

Variations on 'I hate this [the business/networking/life/ myself/etc.]' = 12

Variations on 'I'm not good enough/I'm not worthy/I suck/etc.' = 16

By simply writing these things down as they came up, I was able to hear each thought without buying into its message. That gave me the freedom to give myself some better feelings and carry on taking action.

2. Move it around

One technique that works extremely well when your inner storyteller is speaking in 'you' messages instead of 'I' messages (i.e. '*You're* a loser', '*You* can't do this', 'Who do *you* think *you're* kidding?' etc.) is to change its location.

> *First, notice where you currently hear your storyteller's voice – is it at the back of your head? Whispering in your ear? Screaming in your temples?*
>
> *Next, experiment with putting it in the very centre of your throat, as if you were about to say whatever it says out loud. People often report that when they do this the message changes from a 'you' to an 'I' and the voice changes from someone in your past (often a critical parent or teacher) to your own.*
>
> *Finally, place the voice outside your body where you can have a dialogue with it from a comfortable distance. (If you ever see me having an animated conversation with my big toe, you'll know why!)*

3. Re-dub it

Have you ever noticed that Mickey Mouse always plays the hero?

One of the reasons he has so scrupulously maintained his 'squeaky-clean' image is that it would be very difficult for anyone to take him seriously as a villain. Imagine Mickey Mouse as Dracula, attempting to terrify the heroine by shouting out in a high-pitched Transylvanian accent, 'I've come to drink your blood!' Or what if Mickey had replaced Arnold Schwarzenegger in *The Terminator* and had to squeak the immortal words 'I'll be back!'

One of the reasons why that voice inside our heads always seems so reasonable and compelling is that it sounds almost like us speaking. By re-dubbing our inner dialogue in the voice of our favourite cartoon characters, we can create a completely different experience.

Imagine Sylvester the Cat complaining that 'Nobody understands me!' Or Elmer Fudd bemoaning the fact that 'I'm sooooo depressed.' Not only would we not take their stories seriously, we would laugh at how ridiculous they sounded. And in that space of laughter, we would potentially be able to help them change their story!

4. Comfort it

One of my most successful clients swears by telling that voice inside his head to '#%@&! off' at every opportunity. For those of you who, like me, find that a bit harsh, 'Thank you for sharing' works nicely, as does my personal variation – a gentle, soothing 'Shhhhh...' as if you were comforting a distraught child.

Here are a few ways of practising these techniques and integrating them into your day...

Mastering the storyteller

1. Throughout the day today, listen for your inner storyteller – 'that voice inside your head'. Jot down what you hear as you hear it. At the end of the day, look for any patterns in the kinds of things you've written down. If there's something which has a strong emotional charge, take the time to make up some new meanings and change your explanatory style.
2. The next time you go to the cinema (or are watching a movie on TV), alternate between 'losing yourself' in the world of the film and 'coming back to your senses' and reminding yourself you're just

watching a movie. When you get good at this, do the same thing with your inner thoughts and stories.

3. Experiment with moving your critical self-talk to different locations outside your head. It can also help to externalize it by saying it out loud.

4. Imagine you have a volume control for the voices inside your head. If you're not aware of any voices, notice what happens if you turn the volume right up loud and then all the way down until you are left with the experience of true quiet.

5. Which voice does your inner storyteller use when it *really* wants you to pay attention? Write out a list of positive compliments about yourself and have your storyteller read you the list in *that* tone of voice.

6. Make a list of all the things you know would take you in the direction of your biggest dream. If that voice inside your head begins to scream, practise re-dubbing it with the voice of your favourite cartoon character.

7. Finally, if all else fails, just say 'Shhhhh'!

A little piece of quiet

When my inner storyteller wants to entertain, amuse or even frighten me, one of its favourite stories to tell about me is this one...

I was about to head out to an important meeting. I was feeling incredibly organized, and even a little bit smug about having given myself two hours to get there, which was more than twice as long as it would probably take me. Having carefully gone through my portfolio to make sure I had everything I needed for the meeting, I went out to the car, put my things in the back, sat down in the driver's seat … and then realized I didn't have the car keys.

Not a problem. Back into the house I went. For almost an hour. No keys. Anywhere.

Finally, with time running out, it dawned on me that my wife had a spare set of keys to my car in her handbag. Relieved (and a little bit cross with myself for not having thought of that earlier), I grabbed the keys, ran back out to the car, started it up and drove off to my meeting.

Before I'd driven more than 100 feet, I began to panic. There was a strange clanking noise coming from outside the driver's side window. Worried that I might have a flat tyre, I pulled the car over, got out and found the source of the noise. It was my original set of car keys, still sitting in the lock of the car door, right where I'd left them more than an hour earlier…

So why did that happen? How was it possible for me not to notice my keys sitting in the door of my car while I searched frantically inside the house?

Whilst some of you might make up a story about attention-deficit disorder, early-onset Alzheimer's disease or just plain stupidity, my story is that I was lost in thought – and that being lost in thought is more than just a metaphor. It's an actual physical reality which many of us experience on a daily basis.

You may be lost in thought right now as you are reading these words. In fact, if you're like most people, you went into your head several times while reading my story, visualizing my dilemma or thinking about times when you or someone you know behaved in a similarly distracted manner.

Although there's nothing wrong with this in theory, in practice these little mental excursions are filled with detour after detour, until by the time we 'come back to our senses', 10 minutes have passed and we've forgotten what it was we went into our heads for in the first place.

In short, we get lost in a morass of our own thoughts and stories – lost to ourselves, lost to our intentions and lost to the world around us. And when you're lost in thought, it's virtually impossible to find what you're looking for, whether that's the answer to a question, the next step towards a goal or a better relationship with the person you're supposedly listening to while you're up in your head, figuring out what to say next.

What's the solution?

Stop driving yourself nuts – and go out of your mind instead.

When we go 'out of our minds' and down into our bodies, good things happen. We stop 'listening' and begin to actually hear what is being said to us. We stop looking and begin to see what is really going on all around us. As we become more present to our surroundings, we connect more deeply with our feelings. The chatter of the storyteller diminishes and we open up the space to hear the still small voice of wisdom within.

And when we unplug ourselves from our mental matrix and wake up to the real world, we are finally able to reconnect with our innate happiness, joy and wellbeing in the present.

Here's one of my favourite exercises you can use any time you want to quiet the storyteller and refocus your attention on the task at hand...

The NOW exercise

1. Count 10 breaths from 1 up to 10. A simple way to do this is to silently say the word 'in' for each in-breath and 'out' for each out-breath. Follow up each word with the number, for example 'in (1), out (1); in (2), out (2)' etc.
2. If you lose count before you get to 10 (and yes, pretty much everyone does the first few times they do this), simply begin again at 1.
3. When you get to 10, smile down into your heart and enjoy the precious present.

I often ask my clients to do this exercise towards the beginning of a session if they seem overwhelmed. They almost never want to do it and they nearly always thank me afterwards. In fact, the first few times you try it for yourself you may find it extraordinary how difficult it actually is to get all the way up to 10.

Because it's so easy to drift away into your story while you're reading these words, I have put a little reminder in each of the remaining chapters. Whenever you see this symbol:

check to see if you have become lost in thought. If so, smile down into your body and take the one or two minutes it will take to do the NOW exercise. Each time you do, you are creating an opening for greater happiness to come inside.

Living without a story

Byron Katie is a spiritual teacher with a very practical question, which she asks repeatedly in many different forms:

Who would you be without your story?

In other words, if you could look behind the curtain of your personal history – your daily log of victories and defeats, betrayals and redemptions, triumphs over adversity and tragedies over a lifetime – what would you see?

While pondering that question one day I remembered the following story of a teacher who posed his favourite student a particularly difficult and frightening dilemma...

'Imagine you are dreaming the most incredibly vivid dream of your life,' began the teacher. 'In the dream, you seem to be some sort of an adventurer, and each adventure brings with it new challenges and creative solutions. You experience many wonderful things and some not so wonderful.

'You come to realize that in your dream, anything is possible. On one of your adventures, you encounter a very high wall, so you imagine yourself a rope and climb to the top. In another, you are falling off a cliff but before you reach the ground you begin to fly.

'Eventually, you begin to look forward to each new adventure. Until one time, for no apparent reason, everything seems to go wrong.

'It is dark, so dark that you cannot see your hand before your face. Even before you can hear or see anything, you sense danger. Strange and uncomfortable sounds begin crawling out from the depths of your imagination and coming closer.

'Cautiously, you strike a match. Everywhere you look, you are surrounded by the most hideous creatures you have ever seen.

'You try to run, but your legs will not move. You try to scream, but no sound will come out. Everything you've learned up to this point seems to abandon you and the likelihood of a hideous death surrounds you.

'What would you do?'

The student seemed lost in thought for many moments and the teacher could see a range of fearful emotions play across her face as she lived the scenario fully in her mind. Suddenly and without warning, she opened her eyes and began to laugh.

'I know what I would do,' the student said. 'I would wake up.'

While meditation is traditionally taught as a way of 'waking up' from the illusions of the mind, the practice I have found most useful in unravelling my own story and the stories of my clients is closer to what Tibetan Buddhists call 'undistracted non-meditation' – 'undistracted' because you deliberately minimize distractions; 'non-meditation' because you are not concentrating on anything in particular.

I was first introduced to this idea by my spiritual coach, mentor and friend Peter Fenner. He calls it 'just sitting' and I use it regularly to step outside my story and simply experience life as it is...

The practice of non-meditation

1. Sit for 20 minutes.
2. Don't get up.
3. Don't talk, write or engage in any other obvious external distractions.

4. Let your mind go wherever it wants.

There is no way to get this wrong – as long as you remain sitting (you can move about in your seat if you like), you're engaged in the practice.

Even if the stories of your life never go away, they can become less and less of a limiting factor in your quest for happiness and wellbeing. In the next chapter we'll look at how your stories can create stress in your life and a few of the many choices which will take that stress away...

Chapter Five

STRESS LESS

Angling for happiness

'If you are distressed by anything external, the pain is not due to the thing itself, but to your estimate of it; and this you have the power to revoke at any moment.'

Marcus Aurelius

When I ask people what causes stress in their lives, they are often quick to come back with a litany of stories about external events ranging from lack of money to problems at work to arguments with loved ones at home.

But in fact, all stress is caused *internally* by only one thing – resisting reality. Without a story that says things should be other than the way that they are, we could not experience any emotional stress.

Think about it – does a stick floating down a river feel stress? No – it flows wherever the water takes it. No story, no stress. How does a plane fly faster and faster through the sky? By adjusting its wing configuration to minimize resistance. Less resistance, more speed (and less stress on the engines and wings).

What makes this 'stress as resistance' model so powerful is that once you really get it, you will see that:

Your experience of stress doesn't come from life pushing on you – it comes from you pushing back!

Now this doesn't mean that resistance is bad. As any weight-lifter or body-builder will tell you, resistance is an excellent way of developing your muscles and building strength – it's just that it's a terrible way of creating change.

Change happens easily when you focus on changing what is within your control – your attitude and your actions.

'Attitude' is one of those unfortunate words which has lost much of its original meaning in the process of becoming a self-help catch-phrase. In the field of aeronautics, attitude refers to the 'orientation of an aircraft with respect to the horizon or other frame of reference' – or as my friend John LaValle describes it, the aircraft's 'angle of approach'.

Used in this sense, it's easy to see how our attitude plays such an important part in lessening the impact of stress on our lives. When we approach the circumstances of our life from certain angles, they can seem overwhelming; when we approach them from a different point of view, we can often overwhelm them.

Each of the 'attitude adjustments' I will be recommending for reducing your stress and increasing your happiness and wellbeing corresponds to the steps of Reinhold Niebuhr's famous 'Serenity Prayer':

> *'God grant me the serenity to accept*
> *the things I cannot change,*
> *The strength to change the things I can,*
> *And the wisdom to know the difference.'*

As you learn to stop arguing with reality, let go of trying to control what is outside your control and make clear choices about how you want to be and behave in the world, you will find yourself with less stress and greater serenity than ever before.

The three types of resistance

There are three main ways that our resistance to life tends to manifest itself as stress in our bodies and minds:

1. Denial.
2. Control freaking.
3. Choosing not to choose.

1. Denial – arguing that things should not be as they are

A seeker journeyed through the furthest regions of the Earth to find a teacher rumoured to know the secrets to happiness. When he arrived at the teacher's mountain-top retreat, he eagerly awaited his audience with the reclusive teacher. Finally, his moment came.

'Why have you come?' the teacher asked.

The seeker proceeded to list problem after problem he was facing in his life.

After listening patiently, the teacher sighed. 'I am afraid I cannot help you with your problems.'

'Why not?' asked the puzzled and disappointed seeker.

'Because the gods have decreed that we all carry 51 problems with us at all times. Even if I could help you solve the problems you tell me of, they would only be replaced with 51 more.'

The teacher paused to allow the full significance of the idea to sink in.

'I may, however,' he continued, 'be able to help you with your 52nd problem.'

'What's that?' asked the seeker.

'Your 52nd problem,' replied the teacher, 'is that you think you shouldn't have the first 51 problems.'

We've already discussed the fact that your problems are only problems because of the story that things should be other than the way that they are – that either what is happening should not be happening or what is not happening should be happening.

A simple solution is to ask yourself two questions on an ongoing basis:

a. What's happening right now?

When you ask yourself what's happening right now, that includes what's going on both inside and outside your body and mind.

So what is happening right now? What's happening that we could all verify if we were watching your life on video? What happening for you on the inside? What stories are you telling yourself? What pictures, sounds and feelings are you most aware of now?

How about now?

And now?

The more you ask, the more you will come into the present moment – a place where there are no problems, only internal experiences and externally verifiable facts.

b. Could I let go of wanting to change that?

If I had to nominate a single question to massively reduce your stress and change your life for the better, it would be, somewhat ironically, to ask you if you could let go of wanting to change your life for the better and allow things to be exactly as they are – for now.

While most people seem to initially resist this question, its magic is that it shows up the ways in which we resist so much of what is happening in our lives. We do this with the best of intentions – after all, we tend to want what's best for ourselves and others. But letting go of *wanting* to change something is different from not changing it, and you don't need to blindly 'go with the flow' in order to live a stress-less life. The fact is, intentionality and desire can peacefully co-exist with reality.

Admiral James Stockdale was the highest-ranking United States military officer held in a prisoner-of-war camp during the Vietnam War. For eight years, he was kept primarily in isolation and tortured in a prison with conditions so brutal it became ironically known as 'the Hanoi Hilton'.

Under these intense and relentless circumstances, Stockdale developed his reputation as a leader, an innovator and a man with unbreakable character. Many of his fellow POWs credit his influence and example as one of the key factors in their own ability to persevere through otherwise insufferable conditions.

When asked how he managed to stay sane and strong under such brutal conditions, Admiral Stockdale said, 'I never lost faith in the end of the story. I never doubted not only that I would get out, but also that I would prevail in the end and turn the experience into the defining event of my life, which, in retrospect, I would not trade.'

When asked who didn't make it out, his answer was considerably more surprising. 'The optimists,' Stockdale said. 'They were the ones who said, "We're going to be out by Christmas." And Christmas would come and Christmas would go. Then they'd say, "We're going to be out by Easter." And Easter would come and Easter would go. And then Thanksgiving, and then it would be Christmas again. And they died of a broken heart.'

These seemingly contradictory notions form the basis of what bestselling business author Jim Collins calls 'the Stockdale Paradox'. In order to succeed in the face of seemingly insurmountable odds, you must:

> *Retain faith that you will prevail in the end, regardless of the difficulties.*

And at the same time:

> *Confront the most brutal facts of your current reality, whatever they might be.*

It is not hope that hurts, but expectation. 'Expecting' something that is outside your control is a recipe for suffering. Yet hope – the belief in the possibility that tomorrow can be better than today – carries with it the energy and inspiration to make it so.

In the words of Winston Churchill:

'If you're going through hell, be sure to keep going.'

Choosing faith

1. Think of a situation you are currently facing that feels almost too much for you to handle.

2. Make an inventory of all the relevant details of your current reality. Be sure to stick to the facts, making things neither better nor worse than you find them.

> 3. If you knew that everything was going to turn out
>   right in the end, what would you be inspired to do
>   today to reach your goals?

2. Control freaking – trying to control what is outside your control

In one of the first self-help books ever written (around 2,000 years ago), the Stoic philosopher Epictetus began his *Enchiridion* with these words:

> *'Happiness and freedom begin with a clear understanding of one principle – some things are within your control and some things are not.'*

Yet if you got out of bed this morning, it's a safe bet you have already tried to control at least a few dozen things you can't control today – even if you're reading this book just after breakfast.

Notice how many of these things you tried to exert some control over in the past 24 hours:

- *What your partner or children said or did.*
- *The behaviour of other drivers or commuters on the way to work.*
- *Someone at work's opinion of you.*
- *How something you've already done works out.*

While interviewing Olympic rowers at the 1996 Olympics, sports broadcaster Charlie Jones interviewed a number of the competing athletes. Any time he asked them a question about something which was outside their control (like the weather, the strengths and weaknesses of their opponents or what might go wrong during a race), the Olympians would respond with the phrase 'That's outside my boat.'

By refusing to focus on anything which was beyond their control, these athletic champions were able to bring all their resources to bear on what was within their control – everything from their physiology, mental maps and story to the actions that they took preparing for and competing in the actual event.

In my own life, I've found that focusing exclusively on what's 'in my boat' not only increases my effectiveness, but often eliminates stress altogether.

Here's a simple way to put this strategy into action:

The serenity record

1. As you go about your day today, stick a little note on the inside cover of this book or in your pocket. Draw a line down the middle of the paper.
2. Every time you exert effort or direct a thought toward something you can't control, make a little mark on the left side of the line; each time you focus on what is within your control or use the power you have to change something for the better, make a little mark on the right side of the line.
3. At the end of the day, review your 'serenity record'. What did you learn about yourself? About your work and life? About what you can control and what you cannot?

---

3. Choosing not to choose
How to be a victim of circumstance

A third type of stress in our lives is the result of feeling as though you have no choice about something. As soon as you recognize the choices inherent in any situation, you regain a sense of being in control – and the feeling of stress will begin to disappear. The more you focus on these choices, the greater the sense of wellbeing and control you will experience.

Here are three types of choice you can always make, regardless of what is happening around you:

a. Choosing how to be

On paper, I had a very happy childhood. I was loved, we had a nice home and whatever things my parents may have found difficult to deal with in their lives were handled in a way that kept us away from any sense of external stress. And yet I was miserable, depressed and at times suicidal for large periods of that time.

My best friend had a more difficult childhood. His parents divorced when he was still quite young and his older brother was killed in a car crash when he was 15. He lived in a 'double-wide' trailer house and the money that had been put aside to send him to college had disappeared into the monthly expenses years before he was able to use it. Yet he was happy, positive and cheerful throughout.

At that time I did not yet know that how I chose to be was up to me and consequently I felt a victim of my moods. My friend didn't know about his power to choose, but his 'default' was simply inclined towards the positive. Now we are both aware of the power within us – and while we don't always choose to be happy, peaceful, accepting and kind, we do so enough of the time to take most of what life throws at us in our stride. (And on occasion to throw the stuff we don't want to keep back!)

b. Choosing how to see

Unlike road maps, which must accurately reflect the territory they describe in order to be of use, our mental maps actually recreate the territory as they are describing it. Since these maps often become self-fulfilling prophecies, we can change our experience *of* the world (and ultimately the world itself) by changing the way we choose to see it.

In other words:

Over time, the map becomes the territory.

The way we choose to see our life will have a dramatic impact on the way our life turns out to be. If you see the world as a friendly place, you'll tend to notice the ways in which things work out for the best. Because you're looking for 'friendly' things to happen, you're that much more likely to find them. At times, you may even create them with your intention and your actions.

Here are just a few of the 'ways of seeing' available to us at any moment:

friendly or unfriendly
good or evil
malicious or well-intended
by design or at random
mean-spirited or frightened
stupid or misinformed.

c. Choosing what to do (or not do)

An actress client once called me in a dither, claiming she was 'stressed to the eyeballs' because she was being bossed around on set by a famously belligerent director. I asked her why she put up with it, and she said, 'I have no choice – he's the director!'

I told her the following story:

One day Zeus was sitting atop Mount Olympus when he saw a beautiful doe being chased by an angry stag. She was heading towards the safety of the forest, but the king of all the gods could see that the stag was too close behind her. He immediately thought to cast a lightning bolt through the heart of the stag, but decided to wait and see how the drama would play out.

A few moments later the stag stopped suddenly and turned away from the doe. Zeus caught sight of a huge grey wolf coming into view at full speed. The wolf and the stag battled for what seemed like hours until finally the wolf slunk away, defeated.

Immediately the doe came to the side of the stag, nuzzling his wounds and gently guiding him on towards the safety of the forest.

I then suggested the actress make the following three choices:

1. How she wanted to be in relation to the situation at work – i.e. her physiological state.
2. How she wanted to 'see' the situation – i.e. her angle of approach.

3. What (if anything) she wanted to do.

The following week, she phoned to tell me that she had first chosen to be centred and strong on set the next day and to do that had used some of the same tools I've shared with you in this book. She had then chosen to see the director as 'scared' instead of 'angry'.

By making these simple choices, she felt able to neither fight back nor slink away when he confronted her but simply to listen to him with her full attention and then do as he asked. At the end of the day, the director came up to her and apologized for his behaviour, something a nearby crew member claimed he had never seen happen before.

Here's a quick experiment you can do any time you're feeling like a victim of your own life:

1. Think of a situation you have been finding stressful. If you knew it was up to you, how would you choose to be in relation to that situation today?

2. On a piece of paper, make a list of all the ways this situation is 'bad for you'. Now turn the paper over and make a list of at least as many ways in which the situation could be seen as 'good for you'. Take a look at each side of the paper in turn and notice how you feel. Whose side are you going to take? Which way are you going to choose to see the situation?

3. When you have decided how you want to be in yourself and how you want to see the situation, choose whether or not to take action at this time. If you do decide to take action, do it within the next 24 hours if at all possible.

Of course, when you're in the midst of anxiety, overwhelm or even panic, it can be difficult to remember that you always have a choice. That's why in our next chapter together we will explore some additional ways of mastering our response to what happens when our lives seem to be spinning out of control...

Chapter Six

OVERCOMING ANXIETY

Four magic words to a balanced life

*'Words were originally magic, and to this day words have
retained much of their ancient magical power.'*
Sigmund Freud

One of the things which has always impressed me about my
wife is her equanimity – her ability to treat life's ups and
downs with relative calm, becoming neither a diva when
times are good nor an ogre when times are hard. When I
asked her the secret to her authentically peaceful demeanour,
she told me that whenever she felt herself cruising out of
control, soaring too high or flying too low, she repeated four
simple words that always brought her back to centre.

To my amazement, they were the same four words I had
first read in a story about the secret to stepping off life's
rollercoaster many years earlier. The story goes something
like this...

Once upon a time there was a great king, who recognized that
the more powerful he became, the more important it was that
he avoided the kind of impulsive action that can accompany

both life's highs and life's lows. He tasked his council of wisdom to devise some means of reminding him that his best self lay in the middle path between laughter and tears, joy and sorrow, high and low.

Soon they returned to him with a red-jewelled ring. Inscribed beneath the stone, the wise councillors told him, was a magical incantation. If you found yourself drunk with the giddiness of success, it would sober you up and enable you to remain wise; if you found yourself lost in the hopelessness of despair, it would bring you hope and courage.

Before the king had a chance to look beneath the stone and read the incantation, he found himself transported as if by magic to a room filled with the sound of the most beautiful voices he had ever heard. The king was quickly hypnotized by the voices' siren call and he began to follow wherever they led. Just as the enchanting voices were about to lead him over the edge of a cliff, the jewel on his ring began to glow, and in its light he read for the first time the magical incantation:

This too will pass.

Instantly the king regained his senses, saw the voices for what they were and turned his back on them. But no sooner had he done so than he found himself once again magically transported. This time he was trapped upon a battlefield, his men lying dead or wounded, his kingdom all but lost. A lone rider was charging towards him, sword drawn. Just as the king was about to resign himself to his fate, the jewel on his ring once more began to glow and he again read the incantation:

This too will pass.

Suddenly emboldened by hope, the king found a new strength and knocked the rider from his mount. Rallying his remaining troops, he turned the tide of the battle, saving the kingdom and all who dwelled within.

Like the king, you have the power within you to balance your perceptions and live free from your fantasies and nightmares. But you'll need to find your own way to access that power and you can only ever do that right here, right now.

Finding the moment

I was feeling out of sorts and a bit run-down one rainy day recently, so I drove over to see my local doctor. She looked at me and asked what I thought was a very unusual question: 'Are you having a really good week?'

As I had just closed several deals which meant that in theory I could pretty much take the rest of the year off, I said, 'Yes, I suppose I am.'

'I thought so,' she said. 'I've never seen you this stressed.'

What was interesting to me about that exchange was that it hadn't occurred to me that I could get just as worked up about things going well in my life as about things going poorly.

When I looked at the elements common to both scenarios, the connection became clear – whether things seem to be going extremely poorly or extremely well, my focus was on the future, not the moment – and the future (over which we have no direct control) can be a very anxious place in which to live. The only moment we have any real control over is this one – and of course, this one right now.

As I drove home in the rain, lost in thought, I heard the unmistakable sound of a car skidding towards me across the tarmac. I snapped out of my thought trance, slammed on my own brakes and mercifully everyone was completely fine.

Better still, I had found the moment (you know, this one) – and in just a few moments, all the anxiety I had been feeling dissipated and was replaced by a gentle 'background bliss'.

I have been fairly solidly grounded in the moment (it's happening right now) since then and have reaped the benefits of relatively stress-free living (despite each of my children coming down with the flu in the space of the last 72 hours).

But as I sat down to write today, it occurred to me that narrowly avoiding a car accident, useful though it was for me in finding the moment (are you here yet?), was not a terribly practical experiment to suggest to others. So instead, I've filled this chapter with some of my favourite non-life-threatening ways to find the moment, overcome anxiety and live out beyond the edge of fear...

Spinning your fears

*'Let the great world spin for ever down
the ringing grooves of change.'*

Alfred, Lord Tennyson

Our nervous systems are conditioned to create stability but to notice change. This is a part of our tremendous adaptability as human beings and frees our conscious attention up to be able to notice difference.

As a part of his ongoing innovation in the art and science of personal change, Dr Richard Bandler has developed a simple technique called 'spinning' that makes use of this natural functioning of the nervous system to reduce bad feelings and amplify good ones.

Here's an abbreviated transcript of how I used it with a caller on my radio show who wanted to feel less anxiety and more happiness in her life:

Me: Where do you feel anxiety in your body?

Caller: Everywhere, I guess. I just feel scared and I don't know what I'm scared of.

Me: I'm not so worried about what you're scared of – do you feel any fear in your body right now?

C: No, not right now.

Me: Could you scare yourself just a little bit? Go on, think about the future … can you bring up just a little bit of fear right now?

C: Yes.

Me: Where in your body does it start – where are you first aware of it?

C: I think in my head.

Me: And where does it go?

C: Down my back.

Me: Great. Now, in order for you to keep feeling a feeling it has to keep moving. So if it starts in your head and goes down your back – where does it go next? Back up to the top of your head?

C: It comes back to my chest.

Me: OK, and does it spin towards you or away from you?

C: Towards me.

Me: Towards you – great. Now here's what I'm going to ask you to do. I want you to imagine you're pulling the spinning fear out of your body so you can see it in front of you. You can see it spinning towards you but it's all happening in front of your body right now.

C: OK.

Me: Now, I want you to turn it upside down so now it's spinning the other way, so that it's spinning away from you.

C: Right.

Me: What's your favourite colour?

C: Um ... pink.

Me: OK, I want you to make it pink. So it's pink and it's spinning away from you and I want you to put it right back inside your body now. Put it back inside your body so you can feel it spinning down through your chest and up your back, up to the top of your head and back down your chest and it's spinning away from you and it's a lovely pink colour. How does that feel?

C: (*surprised and laughing a bit*) It feels great!

Me: OK, so now I want you to spin it faster and faster ... how does it feel the faster you spin it?

C: (*with great sincerity*) It feels great...

Me: And I want you to take that great feeling and let it spread from the top of your head right down to the tips of your toes right out to the edges of your fingertips, and the more you spin the feeling, the easier it will be for you to have this feeling any time you want just by taking control of it – because it's not just a feeling, it's *your* feeling...

We have so many theories about 'why we feel this' or 'why we feel that' and 'what we need to do about it', but sometimes the simplest thing to do is to just step right back into your body and take control.

Here's how you can begin to play with this technique for yourself...

Be your own 'spin doctor'

1. Think about something that makes you feel angry, sad or fearful.
2. Notice where in your body the feeling starts. Where is the very first place that you're aware of feeling that way?
3. Now, notice where the feeling moves to next. Does it go up, down, left, right or in some other direction? (In order for you to feel a feeling it has to be moving – otherwise the nerves habituate and we don't feel them any more!)
4. When you've identified where the feeling begins and where it moves to, notice which direction it is spinning. (If it doesn't feel as though it is spinning, ask yourself which way it would be spinning if it was. This could be towards you or away from you on a vertical, horizontal or even diagonal plane.)
5. Next, imagine pulling the feeling out of your body so it continues to spin in front of you. Turn it upside down so that it is now spinning in the opposite direction. If you like, imagine it being your favourite colour.
6. Now pull the 'new and improved' feeling back into your body, continuing to spin it in the new direction. The faster you spin it, the better it will feel.
7. Any time you begin to feel the old feeling, you can simply reverse the direction of the spin and take control!

> You can use this same technique to amplify a good feeling – simply notice the direction of the spin, add some colour, make it bigger and spin it faster.

When panic attacks

When I first learned NLP, I worked in a more directly therapeutic role than I do now. For whatever reason, I wound up seeing a lot of clients who had 'panic attacks'. The structure of a panic attack is a curious thing. In nearly every case I came across, there was a defining incident – a time when specific things had been truly painful and the person felt out of control.

The actual panic attacks, however, came any time the person felt what they believed to be the *onset* of another 'out-of-control' experience. In other words, what created the panic was the attempt to prevent it from happening. It was actually the fear of fear – panicking now about the possibility of panicking in the future.

I remember one particular client who came to me with such bad panic attacks that she arrived at my office lying down on the back seat of her boyfriend's car with a coat over her head. I asked her to come in, gave her a cup of tea and then told her I was taking a poll and needed to know the answer to a very important question: what are the two silliest words in the English language?

After a bit of confusion and some curious thought, she came up with the words 'French fry' and 'parka'. When it came time to take her case history, I asked her to tell me all about her problem with one caveat – instead of the phrase 'panic attack', which I explained was much too scary a term for me, she was to substitute the word 'French fry'. Instead of telling me about the out-of-control feeling, would she mind substituting the word 'parka'?

We then had a fascinating, fun and funny time discussing how many times a week she had 'French fries' and what it was about 'French fries' she found most scary, and eventually I had her tell me about her first 'French fry'.

In addition, she talked about that horrible 'parka' feeling and how whenever she felt herself begin to 'parka' she would immediately begin having a 'French fry'.

Sometimes when I tell this story people think I was being disrespectful, but think about this – for two years this woman had been unable to leave her flat without a coat over her head, and within 10 minutes she was laughing about it. She was beginning to access her own good feelings in relation to the problem situation – and those good feelings would be the key to her finding her own solutions.

Here is an exercise you can do to notice the incredible difference introducing good feelings into 'bad' situations can make. Be kind to yourself by doing it with something that's only a little bit uncomfortable until you get the hang of it – if you're dealing with something really traumatic, I recommend you only do this with a qualified (and open-minded!) helping professional.

Mickey Mouse therapy

1. Choose something you would like to feel better about in your life. On a scale from 1 to 10, where 1 is awful/terrible/helpless and 10 is wonderful and completely resourceful, how do you feel in relation to it?
2. Talk out loud about it for at least three minutes in a high, squeaky 'Mickey Mouse' voice. Be sure to really go for it – 'slightly squeaky' won't do the trick.

If you feel silly talking in a Mickey Mouse voice, you might hop about on one leg instead. If that still feels too silly for something as serious as your problem, talk in the Mickey Mouse voice while hopping about on one leg!

3. Notice what's different when you think about the situation now. How do you feel about it on a scale from 1 to 10?

What you're really afraid of...

'All fear is the fear that unhappiness will happen.'
Bruce Di Marsico

I used to be deathly afraid of three things: investing, heights and commitment (to anything!). When I began to consider the radical idea that we are not so much afraid of what might happen to us as of how we think we will feel about what will happen to us, I looked more deeply at what had at first seemed straightforward.

When I first went inside and listened to my fearful thoughts, I realized that I was afraid of investing because I thought I might lose all my money and have to beg on the streets. I was afraid of heights because I thought I might lose control and jump. I was afraid of commitment because I thought I might miss out on something better which came along later.

Yet as I listened more closely to my inner stories, I realized that what I was really afraid of was the potential embarrassment and humiliation of losing all my money and winding up on the streets. I was frightened of all the pain I would cause my loved ones if I lost control, and I was terrified that if I made a commitment and then something seemingly better came along, I would feel stupid and kick myself for the rest of my life.

The moment I realized that what I was really afraid of was my own feelings of unhappiness, I knew exactly what to do. Here's how it works:

The more you are willing to feel good *about* whatever it is that you're feeling, the happier you get to feel. The more conditions you put on your good feelings and happiness, the fewer good feelings you get to feel. The choice, as always, is yours.

Feeling good about feeling bad

1. Tune in to how you're feeling in your body right now.
2. Whatever it is that you are feeling, could you love or appreciate the feeling exactly as it is?
3. If not, could you love or appreciate yourself for feeling the feeling?
4. If not, could you love or appreciate yourself for not being willing or able to love or appreciate yourself for feeling the feeling?
5. Continue on 'up the ladder' of perception until you are feeling a genuine sense of love or appreciation for some aspect of whatever you are experiencing now.

Know fear

'Fear is a habit – I am not afraid.'
Aung San Suu Kyi, former President of Burma

Having explored the fear of unhappiness for many years now, I've come to realize that while we can reduce our fear with techniques, dispute it with our minds and confront it with our actions, there is a simpler and much more difficult point of view:

99.9 per cent of fear isn't really fear – it's superstition.

We have been taught since we were little children that fear is necessary to keep us safe and to motivate us to move forward. In fact, it is a poor substitute for knowledge, intuition and inspiration.

Knowledge of what would happen if we were hit by a car is more than enough to get most of us to look both ways before we cross the street, even if we no longer hear our parents' voices ringing in our ears to 'stay back'. Our intuitive awareness of danger will let us know not to trust the smiling stranger even while our love/hate relationship with fear tries to confuse the issue. And the inspiration to live a life we love will carry us forward long after the adrenaline burst from fearing a life we hate has burned out.

Knowing this doesn't mean you won't ever feel fear again – old conditioning tends not to disappear overnight. It just means that you don't have to be afraid.

I invite you to use whatever is going on in your life right now to begin a fear-less experiment:

For the next few days (or weeks, or even months), choose to live as if fear is completely unnecessary. When you are about to do something, ask yourself if it is coming from fear or not, and if it's from fear, don't do it. If you're not sure what to do, ask yourself what you would do if you were not afraid and do that.

Be kind to yourself along the way – the fear-less path is not always an easy one to travel, especially at first. But after you've been on it for a while, it's difficult to go back to living the other kind of life...

Chapter Seven

BEHAVIOURAL PROZAC™

The art of staying 'whelmed'

Main Entry: *de·pres·sion*
Pronunciation: *di-'pre-sh&n, dE-*
Function: *noun*
Date: *14th century*
(1) : a state of feeling sad : DEJECTION (2) : a psychoneurotic or psychotic disorder marked especially by sadness, inactivity, difficulty in thinking and concentration, a significant increase or decrease in appetite and time spent sleeping, feelings of dejection and hopelessness, and sometimes suicidal tendencies c (1) : a reduction in activity, amount, quality, or force (2) : a lowering of vitality or functional activity

Or, to put it more succinctly, being in a really, really bad mood and feeling that you can't do anything about it and wouldn't want to if you could...

When I worked on television in the UK, my nickname was 'Crazy Mike' because I was pretty much the only one in the cast or crew not on anti-depressant medication. This was not because I was opposed in theory to the use of medication (or herbal treatments) to help regulate brain chemistry, but because I had genuinely found that the techniques I am sharing with you in this book produced a similarly positive effect on my mind and body.

So, while I will give you some specific ideas and techniques in this chapter that I have found useful in dealing with depression both personally and professionally, everything you have learned up until this point in the book still counts:

1. You can feel good (or at least feel better) at any moment by going to your heart, focusing on 'happy' or loving thoughts, imagining good feelings spreading throughout your body and then focusing on the benefits of feeling good both now and in the future.
2. You can reduce your bad feelings by changing your story, turning down the volume on the storyteller and taking 10 slow and gentle breaths.
3. You can relieve your stress by letting go of what is outside your control (and taking hold of what is within it), loving what is and choosing how you want to be in relation to the events of your life.
4. You can let go of anxiety and feel better at any moment by spinning it backwards and choosing to see things from a different perspective.

Yet so often what paralyzes people suffering from depression is the sense that there's no point in doing anything (and no energy to do it, even if there was a point). Psychologists call this phenomenon 'learned helplessness' – a state of mind where people have 'learned' (or convinced themselves) that nothing they do will make any difference to the outcome of a situation.

What makes the research into learned helplessness so encouraging is the discovery that happiness, optimism and the related positive states and actions can also be learned. By taking small, seemingly insignificant actions in the direction of our goals and dreams (baby steps), we can quickly create changes which not only lessen the symptoms of depression but can also bring more energy, hope and vitality into our daily lives.

What I want to share with you specifically in the rest of this chapter are 10 small changes you can make in your thinking and doing that will make a tremendous difference to your feelings of happiness, vitality and wellbeing.

Consider them an unofficial prescription for 'Behavioural Prozac™'…

1. Be unhappy

I remember a friend of my wife's coming up to me at a party and, with the same cheery smile she always seemed to wear, asking me if I thought she needed to seek medical treatment for depression.

After pointing out that I was not a doctor and therefore not qualified to dole out anything resembling medical advice, I nonetheless asked her to tell me if there was anything going on in her life that she thought might be behind her depressed feelings.

'Well,' she told me, 'my dad was just diagnosed with cancer – do you think that might have anything to do with it?'

'Hmmm…' I responded, trying hard to stifle an embarrassed smile, 'is there anything else?'

She thought for a moment, and then said, 'My fiancé left me. We'd been going out for 13 years and he finally proposed on my thirtieth birthday. Then, about six months into the engagement, he told me he was leaving me for his secretary, whom he'd been having an affair with and who was now pregnant.'

At this point I am ashamed to admit I burst out laughing. When she began to protest, I apologized and told her that I didn't think she needed to seek medical treatment for depression – she simply needed to allow herself to feel angry and sad.

One of the oddest things I have learned in my own quest for happiness is that the easiest way to change a feeling is to take the time to actually feel it. That's not to say you need to suffer – most feelings transform pretty quickly once they've been felt. But the more you push them down in an attempt not to feel them, the more 'depressed' you begin to feel.

Feeling my feelings is neither expressing nor repressing. It is simply acknowledging that I am feeling them right here, right now. Rather than distracting myself from my discomfort or trying to 'fix' my sadness, anger or fear, I close my eyes and focus directly on the feeling in my body. As I go deeper into the feeling, I find to my amazement that within as little as 30 seconds, the stuck feeling begins to dissolve into a gentle flow of endorphins.

This simple trick brings with it an incredible gift – when you feel your feelings instead of fearing them, you reconnect to your body's natural wisdom and experience new levels of guidance, freedom and joy.

Prescription 1: Feeling your feelings

Take some time now to feel into your body. Don't worry about labelling what you feel and don't do anything to try and change it – just tune in, feel what you feel. Stick with it until you notice the feelings begin to change for the better...

---

2. Move your body

There is extensive research on the positive effects of exercise on mood. In fact, Dr Michael Norden, the author of *Beyond Prozac*, has been quoted as saying that 'ninety minutes on a treadmill *doubles* brain serotonin levels'. The problem is that when you're in the throes of depression, the chances of your spending 90 minutes on a treadmill are pretty low. Still, if you think of exercise as both a preventative and a tonic, it can form an important part of your Behavioural Prozac™ prescription.

Joseph Campbell once described money as 'congealed energy' and the same can be said about a static physical body. When you move your body, your energy begins to flow again, and as your body comes alive it becomes easier and easier to stay tuned in to it.

If nothing else, moving your body forces you to pay attention to it, at least for a few moments. And when you drop your attention back down into your body, you might find yourself getting all the way back into your life.

Prescription 2: Move it and lose it

Move your body for at least 30 seconds. It doesn't matter if you don't feel like it – just flap your arms, move your legs and get into action! If you're in a room where you can get away with it, make some noise – scream, sing, shout or blather like an idiot!

Now...

Close your eyes and tune into the sensations happening in your body right now. When you're ready, open your eyes and move back into your daily activity while continuing to be aware of this simple feeling of being in your body.

---

3. Put yourself first – at least for now

Whenever one of my clients begins telling me about how difficult they've been finding their life, the first question I ask is: 'What have you been doing for self-care this week?' Invariably, they get a sheepish look on their face and mutter something about 'having been really busy'.

But not taking excellent care of yourself is more often the cause of overwhelm than its effect. When we feel cared-for in ourselves (because we've taken the time to do those things we know really make a difference to our happiness and wellbeing), we are generally capable of far more than life sends our way.

Perhaps the most difficult and most rewarding place to practise taking excellent care of yourself is in your relationships.

The typical cycle in a relationship goes something like this:

I give in to some request I don't really want to go along with in order to be nice and/or avoid conflict.

I then become angry and resentful as I replay the incident in my mind over and over again, each review becoming slightly more skewed towards portraying myself as the victim and my loved one as the perpetrator.

I then seek to punish them by sulking, being sarcastic or denying them something they want.

Think about it for yourself:

Identify an incident in your personal life you are angry or upset about....

Where did you put someone else's needs ahead of your own in relation to that incident?

How are you now attempting to 'get back at them' for 'what they did to you'?

(Hint: The phrase 'passive aggressive' is usually relevant here...)

We can break that cycle at any moment by putting our relationship with ourselves before our relationship with others. We only prioritize our partner's or our children's wants over our own at those moments when we honestly recognize that it is at least as fun to be loving as to be loved and when we've done whatever we need to do for ourselves that allows us to be fully present with others.

If the idea of putting yourself first still seems uncomfortable or inappropriate, consider that it is nearly impossible to be genuinely considerate of others until we have first considered what we need to be happy in ourselves. In the words of Dr Marshall Rosenberg, the founder of the Institute for Non-Violent Communication:

'Please don't give me anything or do anything for me unless you can do so with the kind of joy a little child has when it feeds a hungry duck.'

Prescription 3: Meet your own needs

1. Jot down at least three simple things someone could do to make you feel loved and cared for. For example:

   Bring me a cup of tea and a biscuit.
   Rub my shoulders.
   Tell me that they love me.

2. Do each one of those things for yourself as soon as possible. If that feels weird and uncomfortable, feel the discomfort and do it anyway!
3. Put your hands on your heart, close your eyes and tune into your body. Ask yourself: 'What can I do to take better care of myself right now?'
4. Do it!

4. Connect with people you love and care about

I have a friend who has been successfully involved with a 12-step programme for many years. I asked him once if he felt that he still needed the programme to stay sober. His reply stuck with me: 'Even if I don't, getting together on a regular basis with a group of friends to share my problems and my victories in an atmosphere of unconditional love strikes me as a pretty great way to spend my free time.'

There is a tremendous urge to isolate yourself when you're feeling particularly down, yet research in the field of 'neurotheology' has shown that a sense of peace and well-being invariably follows the shift from 'me' focus to 'we' focus. Whether you find that connection most easily with family, friends, God or nature, connecting with something larger than yourself is a reliable way of ensuring that your heart stays open and your life stays sweet – in short, a pretty great way to spend your free time.

Prescription 4: Make someone's day

Just for today, make whomever you're with the most important person in the world. Turn off your mobile phone in the middle of the day. Astonish a stranger with kindness. Send flowers to an old friend or a love letter to your partner. Offer to pick up lunch at the office or buy coffee for strangers on a train.

Wherever you are and whomever you are with, ask yourself: 'What could I do to make this person's day?'

---

5. Breathe deeply

Any emotion you are experiencing in your body is connected

to a specific pattern of breathing. Change your breathing (by slowing it down, speeding it up, breathing more deeply into your stomach or even more shallowly into your chest) and you will change the way you feel.

One breathing exercise my clients and I find particularly useful in changing the way you feel about a specific situation in your life comes from the work of Dr Win Wenger...

Prescription 5: Relief breathing

1. Think of a situation in your life that has been getting you down.
2. Imagine wearing a hot, heavy, clammy suit of armour. Feel it begin to weigh you down, compressing and constricting your body.
3. Now imagine removing the armour and enjoy breathing a huge sigh of relief.
4. For the next minute, breathe as if each breath is your first breath free of the burdensome weight of the armour.
5. Check back in with your situation. Chances are, it no longer feels like such a burden. You may even find yourself with new insights and a renewed sense of energy and vigour.

---

6. Stop breathing (but only for a moment)

One of my favourite quotes, for which I have never satisfactorily found an author, is:

> 'Life isn't measured by the number of breaths you take,
> but by the moments which take your breath away.'

In the past week I have had my breath taken away by:

- *My four-year-old daughter's giggle when I tucked her in for the night.*
- *Hearing my nine-year-old daughter singing along to* High School Musical.
- *Watching my 12-year-old son dancing when he thought I wasn't looking.*
- *Seeing my wife coming down the stairs dressed to the nines for an evening out.*
- *Seeing my dogs cuddled up with one another sound asleep on the sofa.*
- *The view out over the valley on a midnight hike with a friend.*
- *A scene in a movie about a family who lived in a lighthouse.*

Each time your breath is taken away by the beauty of nature, love or even a sappy, happy movie, you are born again into that moment – and by taking the time to collect those moments you get to relive them whenever you choose.

While I am not advocating getting all your medical advice from Julie Andrews, you could do worse than make a list of a few of your favourite things – you may find that suddenly you feel glad.

Prescription 6: A few of my favourite things

Make a list of all the things you can think of that 'make' you happy, from the sound of a cat purring to the taste of your favourite food. Carry the list with you at all times and add to it whenever you can.

Whenever you are feeling a bit down and in need of a pick-me-up, read through your list until you begin to feel an inner smile. Let that smile flow through your whole body until you are once again feeling good on the inside.

---

7. Give yourself something to look forward to

While it's difficult to play chicken and egg with your moods (are you mad at the chicken because you're in a bad mood or are you in a bad mood because the chicken's not laying enough eggs?), one consistent element in most people's depression is a sense of hopelessness and futility.

Holding a positive vision of the future becomes easy when you take the emphasis off 'positive thinking' (which is pretty near impossible when you're depressed anyway) and focus instead on giving yourself something to look forward to on a daily basis.

Prescription 7: It's a wonderful life

Take out your daily planner or calendar and put in at least one activity for each of the next 30 days that you will really look forward to. These need not cost money (though it's OK if they do). Plan a walk in the park, lunch with a friend, a trip to the country, a visit to a museum or the cinema – anything which brings a smile to your face and a warm feeling to your heart when you think about it.

If you are having trouble with this one, enlist the help of a creative and optimistic friend!

---

8. Externalize your inner dialogue

One of the often overlooked similarities between keeping a diary and many of the popular 'talk therapies' which have been in vogue since the turn of the last century is the fact that they get you to voice your secret stories.

A funny thing happens when you externalize your inner dialogue – as you tune into yourself and become more aware of what you're thinking, you tend to think less and find nicer things to say.

Think about it – do you gossip more to someone's face or behind their back? (Well, not you, but perhaps some of your less enlightened friends?)

The same thing is true within us – we will invariably be kinder to ourselves when we write or speak our truth aloud than when we silently slag ourselves off in the supposed privacy of our own minds.

Prescription 8: A conversation between friends

Take a piece of paper and make two columns. Write your inner dialogue in one column and your response in the other.

If the comments in the first column are helpful, kind or contribute to your happiness in any way, acknowledge that in the second column with a simple 'thank you'.

In the event that your storyteller is not contributing useful or kind thoughts, use the second column to counter those thoughts with some that make you feel better, cause you to laugh out loud or simply offer compassion for how you're feeling now.

---

9. Have an ordinary day

Research into teenage suicide has revealed that many of the problems kids have in coping with the realities of daily life stem from the fantasies we feed them (and ourselves) about how wonderfully perfect our lives are supposed to be.

When you're feeling less than your best, adjust your expectations. Stop trying to have such an extraordinary life for a little while and allow yourself to have a wonderfully ordinary one instead.

Prescription 9: What do you expect?

The next time you find yourself fantasizing about how wonderfully perfect your life is supposed to be (or lamenting over how wonderfully perfect it isn't), take whatever you're expecting to the extreme until you can't help but smile:

> If you're expecting to have a bad day, imagine what it would be like to have the worst day in the history of bad days – everything bad you're expecting comes to pass *and* your car breaks down *and* it starts to rain a plague of frogs (but only on you).

> If you think things are going to be absolutely amazing, notice what happens if everything good you already expect comes to pass *and* you win the lottery *and* the Swedish volleyball team bus breaks down outside your home.

By visiting the polar extremes of expectation, you may be surprised to find out how much fun there is to be had in the wide-open spaces between your worst nightmares and your wildest dreams...

---

10. Die a little

In the book *Toxic Success*, Dr Paul Pearsall quotes a woman with cancer who was reflecting on what she had learned:

> 'When you're dying, you really pay attention to your family, to the trees, to the smell of a hot cup of coffee... I drank coffee every morning and never enjoyed the smell as much as I do now. When you face death, you realize you could have been paying attention to

all these things and millions more like them every day if you had only put your mind to it.

If you want a definition of success, mine is short and sweet: "Wake up and smell the coffee."'

When you wake up each morning and remember that you're lucky to be alive, it becomes easier to 'not sweat the small stuff'. And when you stop taking your life for granted, you come to realize that the small stuff is usually the good stuff. As Albert Einstein said, 'God is in the details.'

Prescription 10: Wake up and smell the coffee

There are two ways to do this exercise:

1. Imagine today is your last day on Earth. Notice how your focus changes and pay special attention to the things which matter most to you. Many people describe this as bringing a sense of the sacred to the everyday.

2. Imagine today is your first day on Earth. Don't declare yourself to the natives just yet – simply notice, absorb and enjoy the many bizarre and wonderful things this planet has to offer throughout the day.

One final prescription for Behavioural Prozac™...

1. What are some of the things you tend to do when you have a good day – things which nurture your spirit and 'make' you feel good? For example:

   - *going out for a coffee with friends*
   - *writing in your diary*
   - *meditating*
   - *going for a walk in the country.*

2. What are some of the ways you traditionally mess yourself up or bring yourself down? For example:

- *arguing over nothing with your loved ones*
- *trying to get too much done*
- *eating sweets*
- *watching the news before bed.*

3. What are some quotes or sayings that uplift and inspire you?

Based on the ideas in this chapter and your answers to these questions, create your own prescription for Behavioural Prozac™. Put an inspirational quote right up at the top and make a list of three to seven things you can do daily to ensure that you have the best possible chance of making it a great day. Keep it as simple as possible, but no simpler – you can always adapt it as you go.

Here's an example of how it might look:

Prescription for Alex Johnson for Behavioural Prozac™

'The idea that suffering is an illusion negates compassion; the idea that it is real negates wisdom.'
Peter Fenner

Today, I will...

go for a 30-minute walk

read from an inspirational book

limit my 'to do' list to five items (and make sure I do them!)

drink eight glasses of water

give myself something to look forward to

write at least a page in my diary.

You can use the form below to write your own personalized prescription for Behavioural Prozac™.

(If you'd like me to send you some blank 'prescription' forms with a range of inspirational quotes, send an e-mail to behaviouralprozac@geniuscatalyst.com.)

Prescription for _____ for Behavioural Prozac™

Today, I will...

Of course, one of the biggest mistakes people make when they're on medication for their moods is to assume that on days when they feel well they no longer need to take their 'meds'. While they may get away with it for a day or two, invariably the original condition returns, often stronger than before.

The antidote is simple:

The more often you take your Behavioural Prozac™
on good days, the more good days you will have.

A sacred journey to happiness

'Beyond all ideas of right and wrong,
there is a field – I'll meet you there.'

Rumi

In Buddhism, the unconditioned mind is sometimes described as 'the ultimate medicine' – a place beyond pleasure or pain, right and wrong, happy or unhappy. It is the space within which all these opposites arise, and it is the final frontier in our quest for happiness.

In many religions, it is considered the sacred height of religious practice – the presence of Christ or direct communion with God. Spiritual philosophers have long referred to this space as 'the great ground of being', the 'gap' or 'the field of pure consciousness'. In all traditions, it is described as a place of great peace and pure unconditional love.

I want to conclude this chapter with an exercise which could very well change your life, or at least the way you look at your life, for good. It was originally developed by NLP pioneer Robert Dilts and I have used it to make both gentle and dramatic changes in my life since I first learned it.

I recommend blocking out at least 15 minutes to do this for the first time and, if possible, doing it with a partner who can guide you through it. My experience of guiding several thousand people through this exercise over the past 16 years is that its effectiveness increases exponentially when you actually get up and walk through it. By engaging your body and not just your mind, the experience becomes far more profound and the insights it produces far deeper.

I have written the instructions which follow as though you are going to be exploring the context of 'happiness'. Once you are comfortable with the steps, you may repeat it substituting the context of 'depression', 'anxiety', 'guilt', 'shame' or anything else you wish to explore.

Caution

Although this is a fairly robust exercise, it is not a good idea to use it to explore anything traumatic or therapeutic in nature without a qualified helping professional by your side!

---

1. Get five pieces of paper and write down each of the following words, one to a page:

   Environment

   Behaviour

   Capability

   Beliefs and Values

   Identity.

2. Stand somewhere with at least six feet of empty space in front of you. Lay the pieces of paper out on the floor in order like a series of stepping stones. (After you have done the exercise a few times, you will no longer need the bits of paper.)

3. Step into the first space marked 'Environment'. Answer the following questions (and any others that seem relevant):

- *Where are you when you are happiest?*
- *Where else?*
- *What do you see and hear?*
- *Who else (if anyone) is there with you?*

4. When you have a real sense of your 'happy environments', step into the second space, marked 'Behaviour'. Answer the following questions (and any others that seem relevant):

  - *What do you do when you're feeling happy?*
  - *What activities do you engage in?*
  - *If someone was watching you feeling happy on a video, what would they see you do?*
  - *What would they hear you say?*

5. Now, step into the third space, marked 'Capabilities'. Answer the following questions (and any others that seem relevant):

  - *What capabilities do you tap into in order to experience happiness?*
  - *What skills do you put into practice?*
  - *What areas of expertise do you draw on?*

6. Next, step into the space marked 'Beliefs and Values'. Answer the following questions (and any others that seem relevant):

  - *What's important about happiness? Why does it matter? What's most important about it?*

- *What's true about happiness? What would be the most important thing for someone you love to know about it?*

Complete the following sentences:

- *Feeling happy is...*
- *The most important thing about feeling happy is...*

7. Take a step forward into the space marked 'Identity'. Answer the following questions (and any others that seem relevant):

- *Who are you when you're happy?*
- *Who and what else are you?*
- *Who are you at your best when you're feeling happy?*
- *Who are you at your worst when you're feeling happy?*

8. Finally, take a step off the last piece of paper and into a space of unconditional love. Close your eyes and take as long as you want to connect with the best and highest thing you can imagine. You may think of that as God, your highest self, your connection with others or simply how happiness connects with the big picture of your life. For the rest of this exercise, I will refer to this space as 'Spirit'.

9. When you're ready, turn and face back down the way you came. Carrying that sense of Spirit with

you, step into the space marked 'Identity.' Once again, ask and answer the question 'Who are you?' in this area of your life.

10. Bringing your sense of connectedness to Spirit and your new or heightened sense of identity with you, step into the space of 'Beliefs and Values'. What seems true about happiness now? What's important about it? Why does it matter?

11. Carrying your connection to Spirit, your identity and an awareness of your beliefs and values about happiness with you, step back into the space of 'Capabilities'. What new or additional capabilities and skills are you aware of that you draw on (or could draw on) in order to feel happy?

12. Still steeped in your connection with Spirit, identity, beliefs, values and capabilities, what else do you do or could you do in relation to happiness? How have your answers changed? How have they stayed the same? What new things occur to you?

13. Finally, take everything you have learned and experienced about happiness back into the space of 'Environment'. Where are you? Where else? What do you see? What do you hear? Who else is there with you? Who (if anyone) is no longer there?

Take all the time you need to let all the learning and changes you experienced integrate fully into you before you resume your normal activities. You may like to make notes about what you experienced, and you may find that insights continue to come for hours and sometimes days afterwards.

As we proceed into the third and final section of this book, we'll begin exploring some of the aspects of happiness that transcend simply feeling good in your body and expand into every area of your life...

PART 3

Feeling Happy

Chapter Eight

EMBRACING YOUR SHADOW

Coming out of the closet

> *'The gold is in the dark.'*
> Carl Jung

I was talking with a client recently about her 'issue' – the fact that she is about to turn 40 years old in Hollywood. Her problem, or so she says, is that she looks about 30 and is terrified that if people find out her real age, she'll become unemployable. What makes her problem even more interesting (and shows how deeply paranoia can run) is that she's not even an actress – she works behind the scenes and could easily become extremely successful without anyone really knowing what she looks like.

What I suggested (somewhat tongue in cheek) was that she took out a full page ad in *Variety* (the trade magazine for the entertainment industry) with the following copy:

> *'[My client] would like to announce:*
> **I'M 40, DAMMIT, SO JUST BACK OFF AND LEAVE ME ALONE!'**

Not only would she get to stop worrying about being found out and whether or not it would mean the end of her career, it might get her some useful publicity as well.

In every walk of life I have ever worked in or visited, people are carrying secrets – deep, dark secrets ranging from illegal activities to illicit affairs and immoral thoughts that they are convinced must never see the light of day. They will often go to great lengths to hide these secrets, sure that the shame and suffering which would be unleashed by exposing them to the world would be devastating.

In fact, nothing could be further from the truth. In my experience, the negative energy expended in constant vigilance and the ongoing fear of being 'found out' has a far more devastating effect on nearly every aspect of our lives than the secret ever could. When it comes right down to it, bringing these secrets up into the light is the most healing thing any of us can do.

One thing which it is very easy to forget is that 'secret' was not originally a noun or an adjective but a verb. 'To secret' is to separate, or to keep apart. If you are experiencing a lack of union, intimacy, love or wholeness in your relationships or yourself, it's very probably down to the act of 'secreting' parts of your life away into the murky depths of your unconscious mind. If you've been doing it long enough, you may have even been able to keep it hidden from yourself.

So how do you bring a secret up into the light?

For years, my own deepest darkest secret was my religion – I was born a Jew into a family that (mostly) survived the ravages of living in Europe during the Second World War. Among the things I inherited was a deep paranoia about what non-Jews would do if they found out my secret. This was not helped by my penchant for doing the very things which Jews 'were not supposed to do'. I grew up in a predominantly Catholic town, snuck off to church on Sundays, went to a Methodist university and even did some work with an Arabian royal family, all the while hoping and praying (not Jewish prayers, mind you) that my deep, dark secret would not come out.

When I dated (exclusively non-Jewish girls), there would invariably come a point where my religious heritage would come up. At that stage, I became a sort of a Jewish James Bond, thinking but rarely saying, 'I could tell you, but then I'd have to kill you.' Of the two women I told, I married one, thereby forcing her to take the secret to the grave with her as well!

What finally made the difference for me was recognizing that while racism (and ageism and nearly every other kind of prejudice you can imagine) clearly exists, the only reason it was a problem for me was because at some level I agreed with it.

It wasn't other people's hate or rejection I felt and feared – it was my own. And as I learned to love and approve of myself, the hate and fear began to dissipate. Not completely, and not all at once, but enough for me to see the sun behind the clouds and recognize that the frightening shadow which I had been hiding from was my own.

An end to shame

If you're ready to bring your own secrets up into the light, even if it's only the light of your own conscious awareness, take some time to work through the following questions. Be gentle with yourself – if you have been 'secreting' these things away for a long time, you may need to clear out a few layers of cobwebs and grit along with them.

Also, be aware that you may not yet be aware of what your secrets are – if you're feeling uncomfortable about doing this exercise but aren't quite sure why, just take your time and remember that the only person who has to see any of this is you...

1. Answer as many of the following questions as honestly as you can:

   What are you most frightened of your partner/ children/family finding out about you?

   What are you most frightened of your friends finding out about you?

   What are you most frightened of your boss or co-workers finding out about you?

   What are you most frightened of finding out about yourself?

   Which of your secrets will be discovered after you die?

   Another way of digging up your own secrets is by completing the following 'sentence starters':

   'I am embarrassed by...'

   'What I hate in others is...'

   'The worst thing anyone could say about me is...'

   This works because very often what we find most objectionable in others is a clear sign of something we're hiding away inside ourselves.

2. Identify your deepest, darkest secret – that thing which you most fear will be found out about you while you are alive or that you were planning to take with you to your grave.

3. Experiment with letting go of at least a little bit of your disapproval of yourself for whatever it is. If

beating yourself up about it was going to make it better, it already would be, so see if you can offer yourself some unconditional love and approval instead. If you're finding that difficult, do the 'Three steps to forgiveness' exercise in Chapter Nine *(see page 131).*

4. Choose a safe space to bring your secret out into the light for the first time. For some of you that may be with a therapist or coach; for others it might be with your family; for some it may begin with a stranger in a bar. Trust yourself – if a space feels unsafe, it's probably because it is, at least for now.

5. If some people already know your secret, whom else can you share it with? The more people with whom you are able to reveal your darkness, the more light you allow into your life.

Why not take all of you?

'What we want to change in others is what we haven't loved in ourselves.'

Dr John F. DeMartini

A fundamental tenet of Jungian shadow work is that when you disown a part of yourself, it winds up running your life. In other words, you will begin speaking, acting and even pursuing certain goals in life in an unconscious attempt to 'prove' you are not whatever your secret fear tells you that you might be.

You will also begin to project that unowned trait onto the people around you and be amazed to suddenly find yourself living in a world populated by people who exhibit that horrible, abhorrent trait and do things that you would 'never, ever, do, no matter what!'

This is one of the reasons we have pro-lifers killing people who support abortion, relationship 'experts' who can't sustain a happy marriage and crusaders for peace waging war on the powers that be.

The flip side of that rule is what sets you free:

Once you embrace a trait,
that trait no longer runs your life.

I once heard a story about a controversial trial lawyer with a soft spot for defending underdogs and a 25+ year record of having never lost a criminal trial.

Early in his career, the lawyer was called in to defend a black man accused of raping and murdering two white teenage girls in the deep South. In selecting the jury, the lawyer asked each prospective juror if they were racist. With the consent of his client, he would only allow people who admitted that they were actually racist onto the jury.

His assumption was that a) pretty much everyone who grew up in the deep South at that time was liable to be at least a little bit racist and b) if someone was willing to be honest about themselves, even if it made them look bad, they might also be willing to be take an honest look at the facts instead of being blinded by their prejudice.

The same is true of each one of us – when we are willing to embrace the totality of ourselves, 'warts and all', we become able to live in the light of our dreams and possibilities instead of the shadow of limitations and fear.

I have played with a number of variations on the following experiment over the years. All I can tell you is that if you are willing to take it on, it is intensely liberating (and often, very, very funny!)

Creating 'shadow affirmations'

1. What is your secret fear about yourself? That is, what would you least like people to find out about you?
2. What trait do you most dislike in others? What is it that other people do that makes your blood boil?
3. What's the worst thing that anyone could ever say about you?
4. Now, create a 'shadow affirmation' for each of the things you have come up with in the previous three questions.

For example:

'I am a selfish bastard.'
'I am a self-righteous bitch.'
'I am a manipulative cow.'
'I am a complete idiot.'
Etc.

As with 'real' affirmations, have some fun with this. Repeat them often. Emphasize a different word each time you say them. Make up a song and use your shadow affirmation as a lyric. (For example, try singing 'I am a selfish bastard' to the tune of 'Yankee Doodle Dandy'... :-)

Many people resist this exercise like crazy, only to find when they give in and just do it they wind up

---

laughing hysterically and losing all their negative charge around the trait or traits they have so desperately been trying to prove aren't a part of who they are.

5. Finally, add the phrase 'Sometimes ... and sometimes I'm not' to your shadow affirmation. For example:

'Sometimes I am a self-righteous bitch and sometimes I'm not.'

'Sometimes I am a complete idiot and sometimes I'm not.'

IT IS VERY IMPORTANT NOT TO SKIP STEP FOUR.

You will lose much of the impact of the exercise should you choose to do so.

Casting a positive shadow

Of course, it isn't only our darkness we tend to hide. Each of us also has a 'positive shadow' filled with our disowned magnificence.

The positive shadow is made up of those positive traits you see in others but think couldn't possibly be there in you. It is the 'hiding place' of your unclaimed genius, greatness and capacity.

In the case of the positive shadow, we can see its impact in our unfulfilled aspirations, our seemingly endless quest for self-improvement and often, surprisingly, in our personal heroes.

Whether your heroes are actors or musicians ('I could never be that popular/handsome/beautiful/wealthy/successful'), Nobel Prize winners ('I could never be that smart/powerful/impactful') or religious superstars ('I could never be that wise/spiritual/enlightened'), we tend to put them high up on a pedestal, ensuring both that we can never reach them and that one day they'll fall from their lofty perch and we'll be crushed.

Now, remember the two 'rules' of embracing your shadow:

1. When you disown a part of yourself, it winds up running your life.
2. Once you embrace or 'own' that part, it no longer runs your life.

To these rules, I will now add a third:

3. Whatever you admire in others, you also have within you.

The reason you haven't yet claimed the greatness within yourself may be a simple lack of recognition (i.e. nobody told you to look), but is often the lingering after-effect of childhood hypnosis.

If the people in your life when you were growing up explicitly told you or implicitly insinuated that *you* weren't great or special or smart or creative or artistic or whatever, chances are you are still living out that belief as a sort of 'post-hypnotic suggestion' in your life today.

Or you may have simply hypnotized yourself into believing it, repeatedly telling yourself you weren't capable of doing what the big people around you could do (usually because at that age you probably weren't).

I first came across a version of the following experiment in Dr John F. DeMartini's wonderful book *The Breakthrough Experience*. It invites you to take a closer look at where you already exhibit those traits you so wish you had in your life, and it will also begin to wake you up from the 'not good enough' trance so many of us spent our childhoods living in...

Reclaiming your positive shadow

1. Who are the three people you most admire in the whole world?
2. For each person, ask yourself what it is about them that you admire. What do people say about them you wish they would say about you?
3. What's the most flattering thing that anyone could ever say about you (even if you 'know' it's not true)?
4. Instead of creating an affirmation for any positive traits you have identified, take some time to look for where you already exhibit them in your life.

Here are some questions to get you started:

Who are at least five people who already see this trait in me?

Where have I exhibited this trait in the past? Where am I exhibiting it in my life now? Where will I exhibit it in the future?

In which of the following areas of my life do I exhibit this trait?

a. Physical

b. Mental

c. Spiritual

d. Work

e. Finances

f. Social

g. Family

Feel free to push yourself past the first three (or three dozen!) times you tell yourself, 'Nobody thinks this of me and it is not true in any area of my life.' In the same way that you may not have been able to find your keys or the salt or even your car when they were right in front of you all the time, your strengths, gifts and genius are often hidden in plain sight until someone points them out to you.

If you really struggle with completing this experiment, you might just be too scared to really look. In exploring this possibility, consider these famous words from author and lecturer Marianne Williamson:

'Our deepest fear is not that we are inadequate. Our deepest fear is that we are powerful beyond measure. It is our light, not our darkness, that most frightens us.

We ask ourselves, Who am I to be brilliant, gorgeous, talented, fabulous? Actually, who are you not to be? You are a child of God. Your playing small does not serve the world. There is nothing enlightened about shrinking so that other people won't feel insecure around you. We are all meant to shine, as children do.

We were born to make manifest the glory of God that is within us. It's not just in some of us; it's in everyone. And as we let our own light shine, we unconsciously give other people permission to do the same. As we are liberated from our own fear, our presence automatically liberates others.'

In the next chapter, we'll explore how 'letting your light shine' works in the real world...

Chapter Nine

NO REGRETS

A highly personal path

*'Make the most of your regrets ... to regret deeply
is to live afresh.'*
Henry David Thoreau

I have two pictures on the wall of my office. One is a
reproduction of the hand of God giving the spark of life to
Adam, an enlarged close-up based on the ceiling of the Sistine
Chapel; the other is a cartoon Scooby Doo poster signed by
the original voices of Fred, Daphne and Shaggy as well as the
actors who voice SpongeBob SquarePants, Johnny Bravo and
Samurai Jack. (I played the villain in *Scooby Doo and the
Legend of the Vampires* – and I would have got away with it too
if it hadn't been for those meddling kids!)

As it happens, one of my absolute favourite things in the
world to do is to voice cartoons. The problem is that for years
I didn't feel it was a 'worthy' profession, and I constantly
threatened myself, my wife, my agent and anyone else who
would listen that at any moment I was going to go off, quit
the business and do something worthwhile with my life.

The situation came to a head a few years ago when I was
on the phone with an old friend. I was telling him about a
fantastic audition I had just been on to play a cartoon mouse

in a children's television series when he asked me if I wanted to leave immediately to join him in a risky but potentially ground-breaking peace mission to the Middle East.

When I brought the dilemma to one of my mentors, he suggested I vividly imagine pursuing both life choices to the fullest before making a decision...

I began by imagining myself staying in Hollywood and pursuing my voice-over career with renewed vigour. In my mind, it was only a matter of time before I would be starring in an amusing Disney series about a gopher named Sven who spoke with a lisp, and children across America would be imitating my comic delivery of Sven's controversial catch-phrase, 'How 'bout those crazy Yankees!'

I then imagined myself going to the Middle East and getting actively involved in the peace process. I met more people than I could ever remember by name, saw more pain and suffering each year than I would otherwise have encountered in a lifetime, and experienced a depth of love and connection that brought tears to my eyes.

And yet ... all I could think about was that maybe after it was all over, I would be able to go back to Hollywood and do the children's TV show!

At that moment, a story I once heard years ago came to mind:

Michelangelo was on his way to visit the Pope when he came across three stonemasons at work on the foundations of the Sistine Chapel.

When he saw the first, a somewhat dour fellow, repetitively chipping away at a huge slab of rock, he asked him what he was doing.

'What does it look like I'm doing?' the surly labourer replied. 'I'm chipping away at a huge slab of rock.'

A bit further along, he saw another workman doing a similar job, but with a bit more focus and intent.

When asked what he was doing, the workman scarcely looked up.

'What does it look like I'm doing?' he said. 'I'm providing a home for the woman and children I love.'

Before he could go any further, Michelangelo noticed that the third stonemason was working as if possessed by joy.

'What are you doing?' asked a curious Michelangelo.

The man stopped for a moment and his smile broadened.

'What does it look like I'm doing?' he replied peacefully. 'I'm building a cathedral to God.'

Here's what I realized:

How meaningful your life is has nothing to do with what you choose to do and everything to do with why and how you choose to do it.

You can exercise to punish your body or to celebrate it. You can become a millionaire to keep yourself out of the poorhouse or as part of your contribution to the wellbeing of the planet. And in a way that I may never be able to explain fully, the joy I feel in my heart when I do silly voices in front of a microphone is the one of the most powerful prayers for peace that I know.

Decisions, decisions

The fear of regret often delays or even stops us from making
decisions as we paralyze ourselves with stories about 'what
might not be' and 'what might have been'. But what's interesting
is that feeling good or bad about what we've decided almost
always *precedes* the consequences of our decision. In other
words, you don't usually wait to see how something turns out
before you begin either regretting it or feeling good about it.

What's actually going on here? What do these feelings
about our newly minted decisions actually tell us?

Earlier this year, I was speaking with a very good friend of
mine who had a decision to make between two job offers,
both of which would make the average employee drool.

He explored the choices in great detail and then, based on
a combination of researched information and expert advice,
made his decision. A few days later, he phoned me somewhat
sheepishly to say that he was beginning to regret what he had
chosen, although his job would not be starting for another week.

For myself, I find that regret (and in particular
'premature regret') nearly always corresponds to not
following my inner knowing. If I've really listened to and
followed my inner guidance about a situation and things still
don't work out, I don't so much mind. I've even got it written
up on the board above my computer as a personal guideline:
'Follow your inner wisdom, even when you're wrong.'

But if I 'know' at some level that something is wrong for
me and I wind up going with it anyways, I almost
instantaneously begin to regret it. And if I don't listen to my
regret and course-correct (by changing my direction), I wind
up with consequences that I will regret even more in the
future.

In that sense, fearing regret is a bit like fearing that when
you look at your compass it will tell you you're heading south

instead of true north. It doesn't really mean anything except that it's time to turn around and move forward with your life.

Treating my friend's regret as nothing more or less than a point on his inner compass, I guided him through an exercise I call 'The decision accelerator'. By the time we were done, he had reconnected to his inner guidance and 'redecided' which job to take. What made the process truly worthwhile was that he then had both the wisdom to explore the potential consequences of his new decision (particularly to his 'almost employers') and the courage to have the inevitably awkward conversations to put things right.

(As a point of interest, he has now been with the new company for nearly six months and is absolutely loving it!)

Here is the exercise so you can use it to make an important decision for yourself:

The decision accelerator

1. Think about a decision you have or want to make. To make this simpler the first time you do it, choose a decision that essentially comes down to one of two choices.

2. Imagine you have firmly and irrevocably made choice number one. Who would be the first people you would tell? What would you say to them? What would you tell them you are particularly looking forward to about the consequences of your decision? How do they react? How do you feel in yourself about the decision you have made?

3. Now imagine that you have been living with that decision for a year. Things have gone well – not perfectly, but well. What have been the good things

about the decision you made? What has not worked out quite as you had hoped? How do you feel in yourself about the decision now?

4. Finally, imagine it is 10 years from now and you are really, really happy in yourself and with your life. What is it about your life that you enjoy so much?

   As you think back to that decision you made all those years ago, how do you think about it now? What contribution did it make to where you are in your life today? How do your feel now about the decision you made way back then?

5. When you've completed those three steps in as much detail as possible, jot down any additional thoughts or insights you may be having.

6. Repeat steps 2–5 as if you irrevocably made the other choice. (If you did pick a decision with more than two possible choices, repeat the steps with each choice.)

7. Based on what you've learned, what's your decision? If you haven't already, make sure you explore the practical, predictable consequences of your decision, both in the very short term and in the future.

8. Take at least one concrete action in the next 24 hours to make your decision 'real'. If your action brings with it an increase in the feeling of 'rightness', take more action; if it brings with it an increase in the feeling of regret, either repeat the exercise or explore some additional alternatives!

Inner wisdom

When we go against our inner wanting and knowing, we may still be able to generate good feelings in the short term but it becomes harder and harder in the long term. Even as we are trying to paper over the cracks in our integrity with 'feel-good' stories and 'happy techniques', we discover the truth of business guru Steven R. Covey's golden rule:

You can't 'technique' your way out of a problem
you behaved your way into.

While that may seem like bad news if you find yourself in this situation now, the sooner you realise you've made a wrong turn the easier it will be to make a right one.

I was in a meeting once where I was asked to give a real-life example of the idea that at some level everyone intuitively knows what is right for them – not in an abstract moral way, but in a deeply personal one.

For some reason, the example I chose that morning was that a remarkable number of women I met who had been in failed marriages at some point admitted to me that they *knew* the marriage was a mistake before (or even while) walking down the aisle.

Suddenly, one of the women in the meeting burst into tears. It turned out she was engaged to be married and knew in her heart it wasn't what she really wanted to do. However, she was horrified and terrified at the prospect of having to tell her groom-to-be (not to mention her family) that she wanted out.

One of the core ideas in my first book was this:

You are the expert on you. While other people may be
experts on how you're supposed to behave, only you
know at a fundamental level what does (or doesn't)
work for you.

During my adolescence, I used to get a gnawing feeling in the pit of my stomach that I absolutely hated. I would do anything I could think of to get rid of it, from eating to exercise to punching myself repeatedly in the belly.

It was only when I came across the idea of 'inner signals' that the gnawing feeling began to make sense. An inner signal is a unique feeling, image or phrase that consistently and unconsciously comes up in a set context – that is, every time you find yourself in a certain situation, you experience that feeling, flash on that image or hear that phrase in your mind.

What I finally noticed was that feeling in the pit of my stomach only came up when I was ignoring my inner wisdom – staying at a party when I really wanted to go home, watching TV when I knew I had work to do, or saying or doing something incompatible with my values and ideals.

As soon as I realized this, the feeling that for so long had been my enemy became my friend and guide, alerting me to incongruencies in my actions long before the world had a chance to teach me a lesson in its own inimitable (and often painful) way.

Similarly, by thinking back to times when I had a sense of rightness about where I was and what I was doing, I was able to identify the unique combination of feelings, words and images that let me know that even if I'm not quite sure where I'm going, I'm definitely on the right track.

Do this for yourself:

1. Think of at least three times where you have intuitively known something was right for you – a real 'no-brainer' yes. What did you see, hear and feel that let you know this was the right thing for you?

Example: Getting married

I felt a complete sense of peace throughout my body and a gentle smile in my eyes and mouth when I

*imagined asking her. I didn't really hear anything – it was
quiet inside my head, which was remarkable in and of
itself. I started seeing pictures of weddings everywhere
and they always brought a smile to my face.*

2. Now, think of at least three times where you have
    intuitively known something was wrong for you – a
    real 'no-brainer' no. What did you see, hear and feel
    that let you know this was the wrong thing for you?

Example: Buying a puppy

*I really wanted to get a puppy but the moment I walked
in the room, something just felt wrong. The dogs looked
gorgeous but it was almost as though I was looking at
them through a glass wall. I felt a gnawing feeling in the
pit of my stomach, almost like hunger, but I had just had
lunch. The voice in my head was going nuts saying, 'Go
on, just get it – what have you got to lose?'*

Chances are you will find there is a sense of ease, freedom
and wellbeing which accompanies the first set of experiences
and a sense of tightness, restriction and limitation with the
second. Whatever the specifics of your own experiences, the
more you familiarize yourself with your inner 'yes' and 'no'
signals now, the easier it will be to hear (and listen) to them
in the future.

Here are two further distinctions that will help you
clarify your own inner knowing:

1. Towards or away?

When I look back over the past 10 years of trusting myself
as my own best expert, the biggest 'mistake' I ever made

came when I mistook the relief of moving away from something I didn't want in my life for the inner ease that generally accompanies moving towards what I really want.

I had become involved in a business partnership that I neither enjoyed nor was profiting from, and couldn't think of an elegant way out. Quite out of the blue, I received an offer to go away for six months with a show that was touring the UK and Malta. I jumped at the chance, thinking to myself that I had 'solved all my problems' in one fortunate swoop.

The result?

Our house was robbed the first week I was away, I spent every night on the road desperately trying to find a television that had more than four channels and I missed out on a great job that would have taken my career to the next level.

Now this is not to say that nothing bad would've happened if I had moved towards what I wanted instead of running away from what I didn't want, but I know from dozens of experiences since then that when you're actively moving towards what you really, really want, setbacks and problems fade into the background in the excitement and passion of doing what you love and loving what you do.

2. Talking yourself into or out of something

Over the years, I have learned that the moment you begin talking yourself into or out of a course of action based on logic or 'sensible' reasoning, it's a sure sign that deep down you already know what to do.

In *You Can Have What You Want*, I share this useful rule of thumb:

> *The number of reasons you have to do something is inversely proportional to how much you actually want to do it.*

In other words, if you have too many reasons to do something, chances are you don't really want to do it. But if you can't think of a great reason to do something and you really want or know to do it anyway, that's almost certainly an authentic intuitive prompting or heartfelt desire.

Of course, all of this inner knowing is all well and good, but it also raises an important question: If we are designed to follow our own inner wisdom in order to live happily, how can we feel happy now if we've not been following it?

How to live a good life

'I am thankful that thus far today I have not had any unkind thoughts or said any harsh words or done anything that I regret. However, now I need to get out of bed and so things may become more difficult.'

Sylvia Boorstein

If you want to be 'a good person' and live a moral and virtuous life, you are generally advised to do two things:

1. Consciously choose your moral code.
2. Do your best to live by it.

A moral code is any collection of clear statements about what constitutes 'right and wrong', 'good or bad' or, depending on the code, 'good or evil'. One of the simplest moral codes that seems to turn up in nearly every religion is the 'golden rule': 'Do unto others as you would have done unto you.'

Now this is of course great advice, but it is in doing our best to live by it that for many of us the advice breaks down. No matter how clear we are about how we 'should' live, actually living that way is considerably harder.

This is why in order to 'encourage you' to live by them, many moral codes come with built-in punishments for violating them, ranging from feelings of guilt and prayers for repentance to eternal damnation and divine retribution.

Yet how much easier might it be for us to live 'a good life' if we changed our two-part formula to this:

1. Consciously choose your 'ground of being' – how you want to be in the world.
2. Do your best to live *from* it.

Mahatma Gandhi famously said, 'You must be the change you want to see in the world.' What if living a good life is simply the natural consequence of coming from a 'good' ground of being?

The way you do this is simple:

Ground of being

1. Think about an area in your life you would like to change. It could be a problem at work, a relationship with a loved one or even a situation in the world.
2. Decide how you want to be in relation to that situation. Would you like to be loving? Warm? Open? Honest? Strong? Direct? Playful? Fun?

   Whatever you decide, take a few moments now to imagine feeling exactly the way you would like it to feel and being the way you would like it to be.
3. Go into the interaction with the conscious intention to be the way you've chosen, and act accordingly.

When we do our best to follow the promptings of our inner signals during the day, we are blessed to be able to go to bed at night with a clear head and an easy heart.

And even if you've spent so long ignoring your inner signals that you find yourself going 180 degrees in the opposite direction of your own best life, you can choose your ground of being and change your direction right at this very moment now...

The 'secret' of a better life

'The day the child realizes that all adults are imperfect, he becomes an adolescent; the day he forgives them, he becomes an adult; the day he forgives himself, he becomes wise.'

Alden Nowlan

A few years ago, a coach I was working with gave me the assignment of forgiving myself each night before I went to sleep.

Resisting the urge to launch into a lecture on why I didn't believe in forgiveness and explain how when you followed your inner signals and acted with integrity there was nothing to forgive, I decided instead to do what I ask of my own clients – to try something out before telling me why it doesn't work or won't work for them.

To my amazement, the very first night I came up with nearly a dozen things I was rerunning in my mind, beating myself up about and just generally hating myself for. This put me in the uncomfortable position of realizing I'd spent so long disavowing the practice of forgiveness I'd never taken the time to learn how to do it.

A quick trip to the dictionary brought me this definition:

for•give
(f r-g v , fôr-)

1. *To excuse for a fault or an offence*
2. *To renounce anger or resentment against*
3. *To absolve from payment of a debt, financial or otherwise*

As I explored each of these definitions, I recognized that the common theme was 'to let go'. This raised two more questions – first, *why* should I let go of (excuse/renounce/ absolve) my anger, resentment and the debts I feel I am owed, and second, if and when I do decide to let go, *how* do I actually do it?

1. To let go or not to let go?

Forgiveness is one of those annoying things which 'good people' are meant to do, which both turns it into an obligation (and don't you just hate obligations?) and disguises the fact that forgiveness isn't a remotely selfless act.

Holding on to anger and resentment is exhausting and can make us physically ill over time, while doing nothing to the wellbeing of the people we believe we are in some way punishing by holding on to the anger and resentment.

Heart researcher Doc Childre puts it quite beautifully in *The HeartMath Solution*:

> *'In the long run, it's not a question of whether [people] deserve to be forgiven.*
> *You're not forgiving them for their sake. You're doing it for yourself.*
> *For your own health and wellbeing, forgiveness is simply the most energy-efficient option. It frees you from the incredibly toxic, debilitating drain of holding a grudge.*

*Don't let these people live rent-free in your head. If they hurt you
before, why let them keep doing it year after year in your mind?'*

2. How to forgive

Several years ago, I began studying with a man named Larry
Crane, co-creator with Lester Levensen of 'The Abundance
Course'. In his public talks, he teaches a simple three-step
process he recommends for everything from healing pain to
enhancing relationships to increasing happiness, prosperity
and abundance.

When I began to explore the question of 'how to forgive',
I suddenly recognized that the steps to forgiveness were the
same as the steps of Larry's 'Cure All' process – and they
work almost as quickly as you are willing to try them out for
yourself...

a. Let go of trying to figure things out

One of the ways we keep painful reactions alive in our
systems is by endlessly trying to figure out 'why' things
turned out the way they did and what we could have done
differently. Now, if you do this in a focused way, in order to
learn from what happened, this can be a very useful process.
Unfortunately, most people do it in a semi-conscious endless
loop of half-thoughts and ever-changing conclusions.

When you let go of trying to figure things out, you are
left with what is – and while you might not like it, you can
finally face it full-on.

b. Let go of disapproving of yourself (or the other person or the situation)

There are only two reasons why people disapprove of
themselves. The first is in order to prove to themselves
and/or others that they are 'good' people, even if they have

done something which might be perceived as bad. After all, if they didn't feel bad about it, people might think they think it's OK to think, say or do what they've thought, said or done.

The second reason is in order to motivate themselves to behave differently in the future. This is the legacy of generations of well-meaning parents and teachers motivating their children and charges with threats of punishment and promises of reward. But in the end, not only does this type of punishment and reward-based motivation lead to totally self-involved adults (i.e. the only consequence that matters to them is the consequence to themselves), it rarely works.

Let's take a quick example...

Perhaps when you are feeling anxious, you eat rapidly until you can feel your system start to slow down and you relax. But a few minutes later, that relaxed feeling has turned into exhaustion and you can feel yourself slipping into a food coma. When you eventually come out of your self-induced catatonia, your inner storyteller begins to beat you up so that you will never be so 'bad' again. Your blood pressure increases and your anxiety levels begin to rise...

What happens next?

Do you keep your resolution to 'never overeat again', or do you throw yourself naked into the refrigerator, eating your way through the top three shelves in order to once again restore your system to some semblance of calm well-being until after the next food coma when the whole sequence begins again?

When you decide that disapproving of yourself will neither make you a better person nor enhance your ability to go for what you want, the disapproval will begin to disappear all by itself.

c. Give yourself approval

Even after exploring the previous two steps for themselves, it seems absurd to many people to go so far as to give themselves or others approval for what they believe to be their failings, faults and foul-ups. But perhaps the greatest secret in life is this:

There is nothing wrong with you.

Except for the stories you may be telling yourself about how you're supposed to be, what you're supposed to be doing and who you're supposed to (or not supposed to) be doing it with, you are perfect exactly as you are.

To give yourself approval for being as you are is to accept that you are a spiritual being having a human experience – and like the £50 note that has been through the mud and the wash and a dozen people's pockets, your value does not diminish regardless of what you've been through in your life.

Try this exercise for yourself and notice what you notice:

Three steps to forgiveness

1. Make a list of resentments or grudges you are carrying around against other people or life in general. Notice whether you would be willing to let go of (forgive) each of these in turn.

   For any to which the answer is 'no', ask yourself if you are hanging on a) because it would mean something bad about you if you didn't; b) to make sure that 'it' doesn't happen again; or c) both the above.

   Remember, you are under no obligation to forgive – it's simply a choice that only you can make and only for your own wellbeing.

---

2. Some time before you go to sleep this evening, make a mental or physical list of anything you are mad at yourself for and/or beating yourself up about.

   Take each one through the three steps of forgiveness:

   a. *Let go of trying to figure it out.*

   b. *Let go of disapproving of yourself for it.*

   c. *Give yourself approval – no conditions, no judgements and no expectations.*

When you first begin to forgive yourself and everyone around you, it may seem as if the list of people and things to forgive will go on forever. But before long, you will feel a level of clarity and peace about your life that makes you realise that in many cases, there's nothing to forgive.

It is at this point that you begin to access a new power within yourself – a power that heals even the deepest wounds and gives you the opportunity to become whole again...

CHAPTER TEN

THE HEALING POWER OF COMPASSION

What's so funny 'bout peace, love and understanding?

'It is not the threat of death, illness, hardship, or poverty that crushes the human spirit; it is the fear of being alone and unloved in the universe.'

Anthony Welsh

Over breakfast one morning, I attempted to answer my daughter's questions about what to do if she didn't enjoy the nativity play we were going to see.

After listening to my answer, which was a somewhat garbled attempt at explaining the importance of balancing a commitment to honesty in ourselves with compassion for the best efforts of others (admittedly a bit 'out there' for a four-year-old), my wife began to tease me.

'And if we all just loved each other a little bit more,' she said, tongue firmly in cheek, 'wouldn't the world be a better place?'

Well, as it happens, I believe it would be. Why I believe this, and why I've committed my life to sharing this point of view, may take a bit of explaining...

On a religious school trip to Israel at the age of 13, my classmates and I were taken to a place I have been told no longer exists in the midst of central Jerusalem called the Museum of the Future Holocaust. At the end of our tour of the horrors of racial hatred and anti-Semitism throughout the world, we were shown a film which focused on the continued presence and ongoing atrocities of hate groups within the United States, particularly focusing on the actions of the Ku Klux Klan and the American Nazi party.

By the time the museum 'guide' stopped the film to solicit our reactions, I was so angry, outraged, frightened and confused that I could barely speak. In time, I managed to choke out that if someone had walked into the room right then wearing a Nazi uniform or a white hood, I would have killed them on the spot using any means at my disposal.

What I remember most vividly was everyone's calm reaction to my confession, as if that was the only sane response to what we had just seen. I had expected them to share in the horror of my startling realization – that I would have made a great Nazi. After all, if I could be persuaded to hate nameless, faceless groups of people on the basis of a one-hour propaganda film, then what could I have been persuaded to do if I had been exposed to teachings of hate and intolerance from the moment I was born?

Suddenly I was faced with a choice – to reject my uncomfortable realization that I too could fill up with hate and be taught to kill, or to reject my comfortable ideas of good and evil and begin to see the 'enemy' as unhappy, frightened human beings just like me whose ideas about good and evil had been shaped by the people around them, just like mine.

But how do you feel love and compassion for people you were brought up to hate? Harder still, what if they also really hate you?

Whenever I bring up the possibility of choosing love and compassion, someone invariably asks some variation on 'What about bin Laden? You want me to love bin Laden?'

Asking ourselves to love bin Laden, Hitler or any other world leader who espouses hatred, particularly hatred of those things we hold dear, is equivalent to asking a novice pianist to play a Rachmaninoff concerto. Blindfolded. With one hand.

You learn to play the piano by practising scales. And you learn to choose love by practising compassionate understanding – by recognizing the us in 'them' and the 'them' in us.

The first time I really understood this was when I heard the story of Marge Knuuti, a nurse and teacher who decided to volunteer to work in Mother Teresa's Home for the Dying in Calcutta.

After many hours spent on old train tracks and bumpy roads in the heat of the Indian summer, she arrived exhausted, wanting nothing more than to jump into a cold shower and collapse into a cool bed.

Instead, she was greeted by the scene of dozens of people queuing up outside in the hope of being given the right to die with dignity and compassion. Her tiredness fell away and she reached out to a man whose legs had been crushed in the street and whose life was clearly ebbing away. As she looked into his eyes brimming with love and compassion, he repeatedly said to her the word 'Namaste'.

Many hours later, she asked one of the other volunteers what the word 'Namaste' meant. She was told it was a Sanskrit word meaning:

*'I honour the place in you where the entire universe resides.
I honour the place in you of love, of truth, of peace, and of light,
and when you are in that place in you and I am in that place in me,
there is only one of us.'*

A compassionate practice

'Our strength will continue if we allow ourselves the courage to feel scared, weak, and vulnerable.'
Melody Beattie

One of the few perks of going through a period of loss, crisis and/or suffering is that when you come out the other side (and nearly everyone does, sooner or later), you realize that you are a lot stronger than you probably thought you were. Better still, that strength doesn't leave you even after the crisis has passed.

My first real experience of this came in my second year of my theatre degree when I was placed with a group of my colleagues on probation for the final six weeks of the school year.

Whoever got it together and performed well in the final productions would get to stay in the professional actor training programme and ultimately audition for the top agents and casting directors in New York and LA; the others would be downgraded to a 'Theatre Arts' programme where they would spend their time studying the role of politics in the *oeuvre* of Bertolt Brecht instead of actually getting to ply their craft.

So stressful was this 'sorting' process on our post-adolescent minds that in my year alone there were two attempted suicides and one guy (who happened to be my best friend) committed to a mental institution during this time frame.

While I would like to say I handled the situation with ease and grace, the reality is I spent the early part of the six weeks drunk, following my lunchtime margarita with a rota of happy-hour 2-for-1 specials which carried me through evening rehearsals and, on one or two unfortunate occasions, the performances themselves.

Samuel Johnson once said, 'Knowing one is going to die in a fortnight focuses the mind wonderfully,' and as the day of decision grew closer and closer it became apparent to me that I was not the only one suffering. To my surprise, I realized that if I were to make it through and my fellow actors did not, I would feel their pain as acutely as I did my own.

It was around that time that I was introduced to the ancient Buddhist practice of Tonglen – a meditation which brings compassion to life by asking the practitioner to breathe in the pain and suffering of others and breathe out kindness, love and compassion.

Unlike the advice of most of the well-meaning people around me and my own instinct to avoid my pain at any cost, Tonglen invited me to not only feel it completely but to seek out more of it in the people around me.

With each in-breath, I would breathe in their pain and suffering, anger and loss, sadness and despair; with each out-breath, I would direct as much love, happiness and good feeling as I could find inside me back out into the world.

While part of me thought it was nuts to deal with my own pain by taking on even more of it, the reality was that the more I practised, the better I felt. If I was going to go down, as I was sure I was at the time, I was not only not going to take anyone with me, I was going to do all that I could to ensure that I went down alone.

Recently, I came across a photo I took of the panel of teachers I had to face on the final day of term, posed in mock seriousness like a firing squad. When they told me I had been chosen to remain in the programme I was ecstatic, but I burst into tears of disbelief when they told me what had convinced them was my incredible strength throughout the ordeal.

I didn't feel strong. I didn't feel worthy. I didn't 'think positive' and I didn't 'believe in myself'. But I did survive, and I did make it through, and better still, a few of my compatriots whose own fear and worry and sadness I had breathed in on a daily basis made it through along with me.

What I learned was not only that I was a lot stronger than I thought I was, but that I could find that strength most easily when I used it to support the people around me. And while I wouldn't wish what I went through on my worst enemy, I am eternally glad I went through it.

In the following experiment, I will introduce you to the steps of Tonglen so you can begin to experience it for yourself. As with many practices, Tonglen is far easier to do than to understand, so take a bit of time with this one...

Tonglen

1. Open yourself up to the wholeness of the universe - the space in which birth and death, joy and suffering, war and peace continually arise and fall away.
2. From this place, breathe in the 'texture' of suffering. You may imagine this as a thick, heavy dark smoke. Each time you exhale, breathe out the texture of love, kindness and compassion. Many people experience this as clear and bright, light and refreshing.
3. When you have a sense for yourself of the transformation of energy happening inside you, think of a specific person or incident to work with. This can be a stranger you saw in the street, someone you know intimately or even yourself.

Now, with each in-breath, breathe in the pain of that person or incident; with each out-breath direct the energy of love, compassion and kindness back to that person or incident.

4. Finish your practice by extending transformational compassion to the wider world – breathe in the suffering of the planet and breathe out wellbeing, love and peace.

There is an old Cherokee story about a tribal elder who is teaching his grandson about life.

'A fight is going on inside me,' he said to the boy. 'It is a terrible fight and it is between two wolves.

'One is evil – he is anger, envy, sorrow, regret, greed, arrogance, self-pity, guilt, resentment, inferiority, lies, false pride, superiority and ego.

'The other is good – he is joy, peace, love, hope, serenity, humility, kindness, benevolence, empathy, generosity, truth, compassion and faith.

'This same fight is going on inside you – and inside every other person, too.'

The grandson thought about it for a minute and then asked his grandfather, 'Which wolf will win?'

The old Cherokee simply replied, 'The one you feed.'

Chapter Eleven

THE GIFT OF GRATITUDE

On thanks-giving

'Be kind. Everyone you meet is fighting a hard fight.'
John Watson

I recently came across some unpublished writings by Benjamin Franklin on the origins of the American holiday of Thanksgiving. Apparently, the tradition of the early Pilgrims was to spend days of fasting and prayer to plead with God for relief from their many difficulties and hardships.

One day, when yet another round of fasting and pleading was about to begin, a 'Farmer of plain Sense' proposed that as 'their Seas and Rivers were full of Fish, the Air sweet, the Climate healthy, and above all that they were in the full Enjoyment of Liberty civil and religious', perhaps 'it would be more becoming the Gratitude they owed to the divine Being if instead of a Fast they should proclaim a Thanksgiving'.

The farmer's advice was taken and a day of thanks was declared.

Yet despite (or perhaps because of) growing up in a country that mandated thanksgiving, I've never been terribly good at giving thanks. One of the more infamous stories from my childhood involved my saying 'Thank you for the yucky present' to my favourite aunt and uncle, which, while it does get me points for honesty, seems a bit churlish in retrospect.

Here are some of the reasons I've been taught I'm supposed to be grateful:

1. Being grateful will make me beloved of God
My wife, who is brilliant at thanksgiving (both the holiday and the act) equates gratitude with worship. In this sense, giving thanks for the good things we have is an acknowledgement of God's presence and impact on our lives.

2. Being grateful will make me happy
If you were to ask the three happiest people you know why it is they're so darn happy, you would no doubt find a sense of gratitude and appreciation for what they have in their lives high on their list of causal principles. In fact, extensive research in the field of positive psychology has confirmed scientifically that not only does gratitude feel good, but it helps contribute to an ongoing sense of happiness and well-being in your life.

3. Being grateful will make me rich
Some people aren't comfortable with stating it this bluntly, but there is a general acknowledgement in metaphysical circles that 'an attitude of gratitude' is one of the fundamental keys to wealth. The more you appreciate what you have, the more what you have appreciates, and that is as true with money as it is with love, talent and friendship.

So if I have everything to gain and seemingly nothing to lose by being grateful, what is it that makes saying 'thank you' – and indeed the whole notion of gratitude – so difficult for me?

If I put my judgemental 'I suck as a human being' hat on, it's stubborn pride and ego – the reason I'm not more naturally and expressively grateful is quite simply because people have always told me I'm supposed to be, and like a lot of overgrown five-year-olds, I chafe at doing what I'm told.

But if I put my compassionate 'I'm good enough, I'm smart enough, and doggone it, people like me' hat on, something different emerges:

> *The reason I'm not more openly grateful is I'm terrified of acknowledging how much of what I have in life is mine by either chance or the grace of God, and not as the result of my hard work or 'positive mental attitude'.*

The myth of self-sufficiency

'There is no such thing as a 'self-made' man. We are made up of thousands of others. Everyone who has ever done a kind deed for us, or spoken one word of encouragement to us, has entered into the make-up of our character and of our thoughts, as well as our success.'

George Matthew Adams

In America in particular, 'independence' has long been touted as the most prized stage of development. We go out and earn our own money, make our own way and 'don't have to depend on no one for nothing'!

But while feeling able to take care of oneself is a wonderful milestone in any individual's development, at some point most of us come to realize that there's no such thing as true 'independence'.

Unless you harvest your own grain and nuts and grind them with stones ripped from the ground with your own bare hands, every time you have a peanut butter sandwich you are benefiting from the work of dozens of other people who have made the raw ingredients available to you. (Not to mention the employers and/or customers who have exchanged their money with you so that you could buy those raw ingredients from the shop.)

Anyone who's ever lost a job, a fortune or a loved one knows that when the chips are down, the first thing you realize is that not only do you not have control over what happens to you, they're not even your chips. And what could be more terrifying than acknowledging that everything you've achieved and everything you have could be taken away from you in a heartbeat?

The reality is, it isn't all up to us – but it's not all up to someone or something else, either. When we combine personal responsibility with an awareness of our interdependence, we put the 'I' back in 'team' and free ourselves up to live happily in the world.

This reminds me of one of my favourite stories:

A minister is driving through the country when he comes across a truly glorious farm being tended to by a lone farmer.

Keen to remind the farmer of the source of his blessings, the minister pulls over to the side of the road and calls the farmer over.

'The Lord has blessed you with a beautiful farm,' said the minister.

After a few moments' reflection, the farmer nodded his assent.

'He certainly has, Reverend – but you should have seen it when He had it all to Himself!'

Why me?

Many years ago, I was hiking in the Berkshire mountains of western Massachusetts with four men, all of whom had autistic children. I expected the conversation to be a commiseration of woe, and even mentally prepared some of my own sad stories to share so that I might 'fit in'. To my amazement, they each in turn expressed their heartfelt opinion that having an autistic child was the greatest thing that had ever happened to them.

One man spoke of how dealing with his daughter's illness had led him to re-evaluate his priorities and leave a job he hated in order to spend more time with his family. Another told me that he and his wife's shared commitment to accepting and dealing with his son's autism had saved his marriage. The third man shared how his previously rebellious teenage children from an earlier relationship had come back into his life as they shared in the care and responsibility for their autistic sister, and the last man said that when his son finally made eye contact with him after more than a year of working with him, he rediscovered his faith.

When I finally processed that their common joy was not the product of 'happy-clappy positive thinking' but a genuine expression of gratitude for what seemed to me to be the tragedy of their lives, I remembered a conversation with a client who had lost her baby less than a year after he was born. She had told me that what she came to realize as she passed through her own unique version of the five stages of grief was that having a child had given her access to a kind of love she had never imagined possible. Even though her baby was no longer with her, she could still feel that extraordinary love whenever she thought of him – that had been her baby's gift to her.

I thought of that woman many years later in the midst of a more mundane challenge to my happiness and wellbeing. After eight hours of packing, driving, flying and queuing at airports, my family and I arrived back in Los Angeles physically intact but emotionally a bit worse for wear.

It was at this point, standing in yet another queue with a screaming toddler in my arms, that my then six-year-old daughter Clara decided she absolutely had to have a look at her passport picture. This was a seemingly innocuous request, but in fact would have involved my unhooking several bags from my shoulders and letting loose the toddler who, screaming aside, had already demonstrated her intention to leave no 'Do Not Enter' sign undisturbed in her exploration of the world of airport immigration.

Now it would have been the easiest thing in the world to have thought 'Why me?' when Clara was nipping at my ankles and the people in the queue were silently nominating me for a 'person I'd most like to not sit next to on an aeroplane' award.

But after responding to Clara's continual requests like a six-year-old adult (I believe the words 'I'm not going to do it and you can't make me!' may have passed my lips), I took a deep breath, recognized that my reaction was more a function of my emotional state than her behaviour, and apologized for being mean to her.

'Mean?' she asked, incredulously. 'You weren't mean to me. You're my daddy. Daddies can't be mean.'

It was at this point that the question 'Why me?' popped into my head. Why me? Why do I get to be loved so unconditionally by someone who is all too frequently in the line of fire when I lose my cool? How is it possible that her love and trust are still firmly intact after years of sporadically positive parenting?

There is a notion in Jewish mysticism that the nature of the universe is not one of reward and punishment but rather one of receiving or rejecting God's blessings. When we connect with our sense of value in the world and connection to others and to life, we become like God – we share naturally and receive continually. When we cut off from our awareness of being of value and a part of all things, we become distinctly human. We retreat into ourselves and experience a world of pain, loss and suffering.

Maybe when good things happen to me, it's not so much a reward for good behaviour as a case of an abundant universe sharing freely with one of its citizens. Maybe the reason I have a daughter who loves me unconditionally is to make it easier for me to be a really great father to her. And if you find yourself to be happy, or beautiful, or successful, or talented, or wealthy, maybe it's so that you will be able to share your happiness, beauty, talent and wealth with the world.

When my own father was struck by a car and killed many years ago, I felt more anger, sadness and guilt than I knew I had inside me. Because I did not yet have an effective way of processing that pain, I dealt with it by cutting myself off from my emotions. When my own son was born a few years later, my heart cracked back open. I was so overwhelmed with love that I forgot I 'needed' to protect myself from my own feelings. To my surprise, rather than being crushed by the pain I had been holding back for all those years, I began to feel whole again.

I find it an incredibly comforting thought that it is possible to come out the other side of any tragedy enriched with more love, gratitude and faith than you had going in.

And that, at long last, is something I can choose to be grateful for all by myself.

If you are ready to look for some 'blessings in disguise' in your own life, I have found the following exercise an extremely valuable one...

Experimental gratitude

1. Choose an experience that you currently see as a tragedy but are willing to see differently.

2. List at least 20 things about that experience that you see as bad or terrible.

3. Now, list at least 20 blessings that have come from that experience. These may include positive changes in you, other people or the world.

4. Look at both lists. Recognize that they are both likely to be 'true' – accurate yet incomplete ways of seeing the experience. Choose which list to focus on now.

5. Write a thank-you letter to the other person, God or the universe for the blessings.

In our final chapter together, we will take a look at the incredible difference that being happy in ourselves can ultimately make in the world around us...

Chapter Twelve

THE ULTIMATE EXPERIMENT

The story of Guinea Pig B

*'We are not searching for the meaning of life;
we are searching for the experience of being alive.'*
Joseph Campbell

In the autumn of 1927 a man was standing at the banks of Lake Michigan. His firstborn daughter had died in his arms, his business was collapsing and he did not see how he would be able to care for his wife and newborn baby. His plan was to rid his family of 'the burden of his presence' by swimming out towards the centre of the freezing-cold lake until he died of exhaustion and hypothermia.

But something unexpected happened instead. He was surrounded by light and he heard a voice inside so clearly he remembered verbatim the words it spoke.

'You do not have the right to eliminate yourself,' said the voice. 'You belong to the universe. Your significance will remain forever obscure to you, but you may assume that you are fulfilling your role if you apply yourself to converting your experiences to the highest advantage of others.'

From that moment forward, he decided to live his life as an experiment 'to determine and document what one individual could accomplish on behalf of all humanity that could not be accomplished by any organization, government or business, regardless of its size and power'.

He resolved to never again work for his own advantage, but only for all others for whom his 'experience-gained' knowledge might be of benefit, and to take great care with what he said and to whom he spoke. Taking his resolutions to heart, he lived a vow of silence for the next two years, determined not to speak until he had something truly worthwhile to say that sprang solely from his own experience, not from what he had been 'taught' by a well-meaning but misguided world.

He even took on a new name for himself befitting his role in this ultimate experiment: Guinea Pig B.

What began in a moment of self-described 'egocide' on the banks of an icy lake in Chicago became a 56-year experiment that touched the lives of millions and spawned such 'artefacts' as:

- *25 US patents*
- *28 books*
- *47 honorary doctorates in the arts, science, engineering and the humanities*
- *Dozens of major architectural and design awards including, among many others, the Gold Medal of the American Institute of Architects and the Gold Medal of the Royal Institute of British Architects*
- *Work which found its way into the permanent collections of museums around the world*
- *A life which circled the globe 57 times.*

Guinea Pig B, known to the world as R. Buckminster Fuller, revolutionized the fields of architecture, philosophy and art. He invented the geodesic dome, the world's strongest man-made structure, and through his philosophical work on 'how and why humans are here as passengers aboard this spherical spaceship we call Earth', inspired the lives and work of a generation of artists, world leaders and philosophers.

Perhaps even more impressive than his extraordinary accomplishments is the extraordinary impact he had on nearly everyone who met him. As happiness guru Barry Neil Kaufman has written:

> *'Imagine the impact on a nation*
> *by a happy and loving head of state,*
> *on an army by a happy and loving general,*
> *on children by a happy and loving parent,*
> *on a relationship by a happy and loving spouse,*
> *on a patient by a happy and loving nurse,*
> *or on a student by a happy and loving teacher.'*

I think of this every time I question the value of happiness as a worthy goal. Inevitably, I realize that it is not just what we do when we are happy but our happiness itself that makes a difference in the world. The more grounded you are in your wellbeing and the more willing you are to live life on your own terms, the greater the impact you will have on each and every one of the people around you.

What one person can do

> *'God heard us. He sent help. He sent you.'*
> Marianne Williamson

Many years ago (or so the story goes), in a time of great war and consternation, there was a monastery which had fallen upon hard times. There were few monks left and they tended to squabble amongst themselves. Everyone was convinced their path was the right path and the peaceful ways of the past seemed little more than a dream.

In a last-ditch attempt to save the monastery, the abbot went to seek the wisdom of an old rabbi who was reputed to have great wisdom and insight into the ways of men.

When the abbot told the rabbi of the situation, the rabbi shook his head with great concern. 'It is imperative that you find a way to resolve this situation before it is too late,' said the rabbi. 'For what you do not realize is that among you is the One who will deliver us all from fear into love.'

The abbot asked who among them was the One, but the rabbi would tell him no more. On the way back to the monastery, he wondered who the One could be. 'I bet it's Brother Arthur,' he thought to himself. 'He is kind and good. Or perhaps it is Brother Thomas – he is young but already shows great wisdom. Or could it be … no … I mustn't even consider that it might be me!'

On his return, the abbot shared the news with the monks. While they were startled, there was the ring of truth to what the abbot had said. The One was amongst them!

As they contemplated which of them it might be, the monks began to treat one another with a very special reverence and respect. After all, someone among them might really be the One. And, on the off-chance that each monk himself might be the One, they began to treat themselves with extraordinary respect and reverence as well.

As time went by, the monks developed a gentle, loving quality about them which was hard to quantify but easy to notice. They lived respectfully, in harmony with themselves and nature. An aura of respect and reverence seemed to radiate out from them and permeate the atmosphere. There was something strangely attractive, even compelling about it.

Before long, people were coming from far and wide to be nourished by the life of the monks, and young men were asking to become a part of their community. Within a few short years, the monastery had once again become home to a thriving order – a vibrant centre of light and spirituality in the world.

If you knew that you really mattered – that your life was essential to the wellbeing of the planet – what would you do to cultivate your own happiness and wellbeing? What would you stop doing? What would you do more of? What would you do less of?

If you knew that each person you met today might be the One, how would you treat them?

Be aware that anyone and anything you treat with reverence becomes sacred – and that includes both you and your life.

I began this book with a quote from the playwright and social activist George Bernard Shaw. Here it is in its entirety:

> *'This is the true joy in life – the being used for a purpose recognized by yourself as a mighty one; the being thoroughly worn out before you are thrown on the scrap heap; the being a force of Nature instead of a feverish selfish little clod of ailments and grievances complaining that the world will not devote itself to making you happy.*
>
> *I am of the opinion that my life belongs to the whole community and as long as I can live it is my privilege to do for it what I can. I want to be thoroughly used up when I die, for the harder I work, the more I live. I rejoice in life for its own sake.*

Life is no "brief candle" to me. It is a sort of splendid torch which I have got hold of for the moment, and I want to make it burn as brightly as possible before handing it on to future generations.'

As you contemplate what kind of a vision, purpose or mission would get you jumping out of bed in the morning and forcing yourself to get back in at night, here's an experiment in finding the true joy in life that can go on for at least as long as you do...

A life-changing experiment

1. Imagine that your life up until now has been an experiment. What has it been an experiment in? Examples:

   - *How far can one person go without paying attention to their life?*
   - *How long can one person maintain an intimate relationship without demonstrating respect for their partner?*
   - *How much blame, shame and guilt can one person experience before they self-destruct completely?*

2. Choose an experiment worth committing your life to – your very own 'ultimate experiment'! Examples:

   - *How far can I advance in my career while staying 100 per cent true to my values?*
   - *If I found more peace within myself, would it lead to more peace in the world?*

> • *What is the difference I can make in the lives of others by simply loving them unconditionally and believing in their ability to make different choices and lead radically different lives?*

Some final thoughts on feeling happy now

When I first share the ideas we have been exploring together in this book, there is often a palpable excitement as people begin to experience their own power to create and live from a place of happiness and wellbeing inside themselves.

Occasionally they will ask me whether if they use these tools enough it means they will never feel unhappy again.

Fortunately, the answer is 'no' – I have as yet not come across a lasting, meaningful happiness that doesn't include the full spectrum of experience and emotion. But I know for myself the joy of a life that gets better and better as you and I become happier and happier.

Think about it like this. You've probably seen this classic drawing of the cycles of most of the body's natural rhythms:

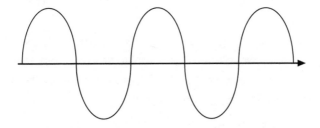

Now notice what happens if you accept the ups and downs of your daily rhythms but you experience them in the context of an ongoing programme for increasing your happiness and wellbeing:

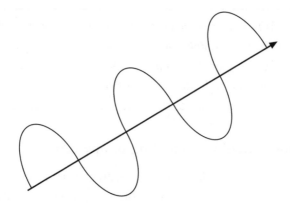

Your highs become higher, but your lows become higher as well. Over time, what was once a 10 on your scale of happiness can become your new 1. It is, perhaps, an unreasonable goal. But in my experience, all the best goals inevitably are.

Here's one last thought experiment to take with you as you continue on your journey...

Take a few moments now to love and appreciate whatever it is you love and appreciate about yourself. You can expand that love to include your immediate family and your close friends. Continue expanding in love to include what you love and appreciate about your home, your neighbourhood, your community, your country, your planet, your universe and whatever concept of the word 'God' or 'Spirit' or 'Unconditional Love' you find meaningful to you.

Now... open up to receive all that love back, knowing that the mathematics of love are exponential – whatever you give away comes back multiplied. Imagine the love that God/Spirit/Unconditional Love has for you. Imagine being loved by the universe, loved by the Earth, loved by your country.

Open up to the idea of being loved and appreciated by your community, loved and appreciated by your neighbourhood, loved and appreciated in your home. And as you imagine being loved and appreciated by the people you care about most, finish once again by feeling – really feeling – the love and appreciation you have for whatever it is you love and appreciate about yourself...

I will close with the words of the person who has taught me more than anyone about love and happiness – my wife Nina:

'(S)he who dies with the most love wins!'

Until we meet,

Appendix

TO BE OPENED IN CASE OF EMERGENCY

*'There is chaos under the heavens and
the situation is excellent.'*
Chinese proverb

While it would be nice to believe that reading this book would be enough to inoculate you against the slings and arrows of outrageous fortune, I live in the real world – a world where nothing lasts, no one gets out alive and bad things happen to good people. (In fairness, they happen to 'bad' people too in roughly the same proportion, a fact that seems to elude most observers.)

This impartial 'karma' isn't noticed because from a very early age we are taught to take things personally – that not only do we have the power to make the people around us happy, but they have the power to make us very unhappy indeed.

But what happens when we stop taking things personally? When we let go of the story that God or the universe or the wheel of karma has singled us out to be flung up to the heights or down to the depths as punishment or reward for what we did or didn't do in this life or the last?

I remember finding great meaning in the words of Holocaust survivor Viktor Frankl, describing a long march in the dead of winter through the death camps of Auschwitz:

> *'A thought transfixed me: for the first time in my life I saw the truth as it is set into song by so many poets, proclaimed as the final wisdom by so many thinkers. The truth – that love is the ultimate and the highest goal to which man can aspire. Then I grasped the meaning of the greatest secret that human poetry and human thought and belief have to impart: The salvation of man is through love and in love.*
>
> *I understood how a man who has nothing left in this world may still know bliss, be it only for a brief moment, in the contemplation of his beloved. In a position of utter desolation, when a man cannot express himself in positive action, when his only achievement may consist in enduring his sufferings in the right way – an honourable way – in such a position man can, through loving contemplation of the image he carries of his beloved, achieve fulfilment. For the first time in my life, I was able to understand the words, "The angels are lost in perpetual contemplation of an infinite glory."'*

When I first read that, I figured that if people could find moments of happiness in a concentration camp, then I could probably find a few in the midst of paradise.

Here is a reminder of the key formulas, recipes, experiments and techniques that will help you to feel happy and cared for even in the midst of the emergencies and crises of your life:

Finally, here is a treasure I personally use whenever I need to balance my perceptions and renew my spirit – the *Desiderata* of German-American poet Max Ehrmann:

Go placidly amid the noise and haste,
and remember what peace there may be in silence.

As far as possible without surrender
be on good terms with all persons.

Speak your truth quietly and clearly;
and listen to others,
even the dull and the ignorant;
they too have their story.

Avoid loud and aggressive persons,
they are vexations to the spirit.

If you compare yourself with others,
you may become vain and bitter;
for always there will be greater and lesser persons than
yourself.

Enjoy your achievements as well as your plans.
Keep interested in your own career, however humble;
it is a real possession in the changing fortunes of time.

Exercise caution in your business affairs;
for the world is full of trickery.

But let this not blind you to what virtue there is;
many persons strive for high ideals;
and everywhere life is full of heroism.

Be yourself.

Especially, do not feign affection.
Neither be cynical about love;
for in the face of all aridity and disenchantment
it is as perennial as the grass.

Take kindly the counsel of the years,
gracefully surrendering the things of youth.

Nurture strength of spirit to shield you in sudden misfortune.
But do not distress yourself with dark imaginings.
Many fears are born of fatigue and loneliness.
Beyond a wholesome discipline,
be gentle with yourself.

You are a child of the universe,
no less than the trees and the stars;
you have a right to be here.

And whether or not it is clear to you,
no doubt the universe is unfolding as it should.

Therefore be at peace with God,
whatever you conceive Him to be,
and whatever your labours and aspirations,
in the noisy confusion of life keep peace with your soul.

With all its sham, drudgery, and broken dreams,
it is still a beautiful world.

Be cheerful.

Strive to be happy.

WANT TO LEARN MORE?

I have collected some of my favourite resources for creating happiness at my website.

Please visit: www.geniuscatalyst. com/happy.php

If you would like to join the Genius Catalyst community and have access to hundreds of tips, podcasts, e-programs and more on the art and science of creating happy success, you can find all this and more at our main site:

www.geniuscatalyst.com

Happy exploring!

Hay House Titles of Related Interest

YOU CAN HEAL YOUR LIFE, *the movie, starring
Louise L. Hay & Friends (available as a 1-DVD set and
an expanded 2-DVD set)*
Watch the trailer at **www.LouiseHayMovie.com**

******

Ask and It Is Given, by Esther and Jerry Hicks

Everyday Positive Thinking, by Louise L. Hay

Everything You Need To Know To Feel Good, by Candace Pert

Four Acts of Personal Power, by Denise Linn

Love Yourself ... And It Doesn't Matter Who You Marry, by
Eva-Maria Zurhorst

The Power Is Within You, by Louise L. Hay

The Power of Intention, by Wayne W. Dyer

ABOUT THE AUTHOR

Michael Neill is an internationally renowned success coach, licensed Master Trainer of Neuro-Linguistic Programming (NLP) and the bestselling author of *You Can Have What You Want*, the *Effortless Success* audio program and *Supercoach: 10 Secrets to Transform Anyone's Life*. He has spent the past 20 years as a coach, adviser, friend, mentor and creative spark plug to celebrities, CEOs, royalty and people who want to get more out of their lives. His books have been translated into 10 languages, and his public talks and seminars have been well received around the world. He regularly lectures in the UK.

www.supercoach.com

We hope you enjoyed this Hay House book.
If you would like to receive a free catalogue featuring additional
Hay House books and products, or if you would like information
about the Hay Foundation, please contact:

Hay House UK Ltd
292B Kensal Road • London W10 5BE
Tel: (44) 20 8962 1230; Fax: (44) 20 8962 1239
www.hayhouse.co.uk

***

Published and distributed in the United States of America by:
Hay House, Inc. • PO Box 5100 • Carlsbad, CA 92018-5100
Tel: (1) 760 431 7695 or (1) 800 654 5126;
Fax: (1) 760 431 6948 or (1) 800 650 5115
www.hayhouse.com

***

Published and distributed in Australia by:
Hay House Australia Ltd • 18/36 Ralph Street • Alexandria, NSW 2015
Tel: (61) 2 9669 4299, Fax: (61) 2 9669 4144
www.hayhouse.com.au

***

Published and distributed in the Republic of South Africa by:
Hay House SA (Pty) Ltd • PO Box 990 • Witkoppen 2068
Tel/Fax: (27) 11 467 8904
www.hayhouse.co.za

***

Published and distributed in India by:
Hay House Publishers India • Muskaan Complex • Plot No.3
B-2• Vasant Kunj • New Delhi - 110 070
Tel: (91) 11 41761620; Fax: (91) 11 41761630
www.hayhouse.co.in

***

Distributed in Canada by:
Raincoast • 9050 Shaughnessy St • Vancouver, BC V6P 6E5
Tel: (1) 604 323 7100
Fax: (1) 604 323 2600

***

Sign up via the Hay House UK website to receive the Hay House
online newsletter and stay informed about what's going on with your
favourite authors. You'll receive bimonthly announcements
about discounts and offers, special events, product highlights,
free excerpts, giveaways, and more!
www.hayhouse.co.uk